SAFE IN HIS CARE

SAFE IN HIS CARE

By Lily A. Bear
Artist: Loraine Wenger

Rod and Staff Publishers, Inc.
P.O. Box 3, 14193 Hwy. 172
Crockett, Kentucky 41413
Telephone: (606) 522-4348

Printed in U.S.A.

Code no. 84-8-02

Catalog no. 2373

for my children
and
for all boys and girls
so that each would realize
that god cares
for them

"Casting all your care upon him; for he careth for you" (1 Peter 5:7).

CONTENTS

1. Lost?.................................... 13

2. The Longest Night........................ 25

3. Snowstorm............................... 33

4. Snowbound.............................. 41

5. Winter Wonders......................... 49

6. Night Visitors......................... 60

7. Story Time............................ 67

8. Across the Ice........................ 75

9. Spring Prowler........................ 85

10. Wagon Car............................ 97

11. Kindness............................107

12. Pride...............................113

13. Plans...............................124

14. Sheepshearing.......................133

15. Fleece Lessons......................139

16. Working Together....................147

17. Company...155

18. Slab Shack..164

19. Happiness...175

20. Summer Twilight..................................184

21. Disappointments..................................195

22. Hailstorm...204

23. Learning God's Care............................213

24. Visiting Bush Mill...............................222

25. Fire! 231

26. Lodgers..242

27. Surprises..248

28. Without Father....................................255

29. The Second Day..................................264

30. Third Day...272

31. Ice Fishing...282

32. Night Chorus.......................................292

33. Vacation Days......................................300

34. Letters...312

35. Moving..319

meet...

Father
Mother
Raymond, 14
Martha, 13
Linda, 10
Rodney, 8
Joanna, 5
baby Donnie

as they experience joys, struggles, and triumphs in working together, sharing, and striving to serve God in their northern home.

The old log house by a winding road
    Looked weathered, decaying, and gray;
"What makes that old cabin so joyful?"
    A bird heard the whisp'ring pines say.

"For when the north wind rages and blows,
    Its joints groan and shudder and creak;
The worn roof of ancient, old shingles,
    Is battered and splintered, and leaks.

"We see where the chinks are crumbled and gone,
    Where the floorboards are warped—they sag, too."
A wise small bird interrupted them,
    "Please, listen while I sing for you."

His sweet notes rose as he sang of love,
    Free-flowing behind aged walls;
Of happiness, many small, kind deeds,
    And laughter that rang through the halls.

He sang of love to the children dear,
    From God-fearing parents so strong;
"This home is welcomed and loved by all,"
    He chirped as he finished his song.

The pines swayed silently as they thought;
    With greater respect they looked down;
Then spread their boughs shelt'ring o'er the home
    Where love, joy, and peace did abound.

Lost?

"Mother!" Raymond called breathlessly as he poked his head around the open door, "Father wants to know if we can eat lunch at ten-thirty today?"

"Come in and shut the door," Mother answered, smiling at her oldest son.

Sheepishly, Raymond shut the door, blocking out the bitter winter air. "Can we eat a lunch at ten-thirty, Mother? Father wants to get another load of fence-post logs yet today."

"Tell Father I'll have it ready," Mother replied, glancing at the clock.

Quickly Raymond left the house, stepping outdoors into the darkness. As he walked toward the shop, he turned to check the eastern sky. A light streak was beginning to show above the tree line, so Raymond knew the daylight of their short winter day would begin before long. He took a deep breath of the frosty air, opened the shop door, and stepped into the warmth.

"Mother said she would have it ready," Raymond answered Father's inquiring look as he glanced up from the chain saw he was sharpening.

Back and forth, back and forth, Father guided the file. "I'm almost finished," he said a few moments later as he filled the saw with gas and oil, "so turn the stove damper shut." Then he turned off the lantern that furnished the light in the shop, and father and son stepped into the outdoors.

"It is lighter out here already than when I came from the house," Raymond remarked. "Each winter it takes me awhile to get used to only a few hours of sunlight a day."

"Yes," Father agreed. "December is a dark month here in northern Canada. Let's hurry and eat so we can get started before the sun shines. By eleven o'clock it should be quite light." Father quickened his steps toward the log house.

Indoors, Mother set a bowl of steaming soup on the table.

"Why are there only two soup bowls?" five-year-old Joanna questioned as she stood beside the table. "Won't we get any dinner?"

"Yes, Dear," Mother reassured her youngest daughter, "but we will eat later. Since today is Saturday and Raymond is home from school, Father wants to start working as soon as it is daylight. I hear Father and Raymond now. Call the others and we will all sit down with them."

At Joanna's call, Martha stood her dust mop against the bedroom wall and turned to Linda who was gazing dreamily out the window, her dustcloth hanging limply from her hand. "If you would help more, we could finish our cleaning in good time. I want to help Mother make doughnuts this afternoon."

Linda sighed. "Martha and her cleaning," she thought. Linda wished that she enjoyed working indoors as much as Martha did. "But she is thirteen and three years older than I," Linda consoled herself. Dropping the dustcloth beside Martha's mop, Linda hurried to the table and slid into her place beside Rodney.

"May I go with you?" Rodney eagerly looked at Father after Father had asked the blessing.

"I guess not today, Son," Father replied kindly. "You need to bring in extra wood for over Sunday, and I'm sure Mother has some other jobs for you to do, too."

Rodney smiled, trying to hide his disappointment.

"I'll help Rodney get wood," Linda offered quickly. She glanced toward the window; the outdoors was beckoning her as usual.

"Whatever Mother says," Father consented, finishing the last of his soup.

Father and Raymond were soon at the barn hitching the horse to the sleigh. In a short time they were on their way. The horse broke into a trot as they passed the sawmill and started down the snow-covered trail leading into the forest. Father stood on the sleigh's board floor, expertly holding the reins. The sleigh flew effortlessly across the soft snow.

Daylight was arriving, for when they emerged from the trees, they could easily see the open field and the road beyond. Before long, they once again entered the darkness of the forest. Only the thin, white line of the logging trail that stretched ahead of them through the trees could be seen.

"Whoa—whoa," Father called, bringing Betsy to a standstill. "This is where we will cut," he announced to Raymond. "Notice all the small tamarack trees? They are just the right size for fence posts."

"How long ago did a fire go through here?" Raymond asked, looking at the old blackened tree trunks protruding from among the small trees that were replacing them.

"About five years ago," Father answered. "Remember the dry summer when you were nine and we had a lot of small forest fires?"

Whin-ee-ee. Father's saw vibrated through the forest.

Crash! the first tree fell.

Chop, chop, chop. Raymond swung his axe, expertly cutting away the tree limbs.

Steadily they worked, cutting and limbing tree after tree.

An hour passed before Father shut off his saw and walked to where Raymond was working.

"Is it going to snow?" Raymond looked questioningly to where the sun was struggling to shine through the gray, overcast sky.

"It looks as if it will," Father answered, picking up an axe to help Raymond cut limbs from the trees he had felled.

Before long the sun disappeared completely. Lower and lower the clouds seemed to sink; darker and darker the atmosphere became. A few snowflakes sifted down, dancing here and there.

"Let's hurry and finish limbing so we can load the sleigh yet today. If it snows very much, we won't be able to find our logs," Father said, swinging his axe faster.

Big snowflakes began to fall more rapidly, making the gloomy world even darker.

"Run, bring the sleigh closer," Father called. "It looks as though we are in for a real storm."

Together Father and Raymond loaded the logs, working as fast as they could. By now it was hard to see anything but a wall of white dancing snowflakes.

Anxiously Raymond climbed up onto the loaded logs, wishing they were safe at home. Betsy headed homeward, her head lowered against the snow and wind that drove against them.

"We haven't had a snowstorm come so fast for years," Father shouted as he guided Betsy between the faint outline of the trees.

When they reached the open field, the full force of the wind and driving snow swirled around them. "We will follow the trees again," Father shouted. The screaming wind grabbed Father's words and hurled them into the storm.

Raymond's eyes hurt from straining to see through the white wall. Suddenly the storm seemed to lessen and Raymond realized that they had left the field and were now traveling between the trees. "Good," he thought to himself, "we are almost to the sawmill."

Once more they left the shelter of the trees to encounter the fury of the storm as

Could Betsy find her way home, or would they be lost?

it beat against them from all directions. They could see nothing. Hesitantly, the horse stopped. Father flicked the reins, but still Betsy refused to move.

*   *   *   *

Meanwhile, Mother looked anxiously out the window into the swirling white world. Where could Raymond and Father be? The storm had come up so quickly. It was only when the first snowflakes fell that Mother noticed the snow-ladened clouds.

"How can they see to come home?" Martha asked as she joined Mother at the darkened window.

"Maybe they are already at the barn," Mother answered reassuringly. "It's always comforting to know our heavenly Father can see when we are unable to." Mother started humming as she left the window and began rolling out doughnuts.

Martha followed her. "Father and Raymond will enjoy these," she commented as she cut out doughnuts and placed them on a pan. "Umm. I can already taste them." Then a frightening thought came: Father and Raymond were out in the storm. Might they be lost?

Martha glanced at Mother's calm, untroubled face, and her worrying ceased. "Yes, God is watching," she reminded herself.

*　　*　　*　　*

When Betsy would not move, Father got down and went to lead her. Taking a step forward, he bumped into something. "Why it's the sawmill!" he exclaimed. "I thought we were past it."

Carefully Father led Betsy around the sawmill, and groping his way, he was able to pass the slab piles without hitting them. "Now it's just open field to the barn," he thought. "I believe I'll let Betsy find her own way."

Father climbed back into the sleigh, gave the reins a sharp flick, then let them hang loosely.

Raymond was relieved when Father climbed back onto the sleigh and he felt it begin to move. By now, even Betsy's dark form had disappeared in the swirling white world. Where were they? Could Betsy find her way home or would they be lost? These questions raced through Raymond's mind as the sleigh moved steadily on.

Suddenly the sleigh stopped. Once more, Father climbed down to lead Betsy, but this time he stumbled against the fence. Guessing his directions correctly, Father headed toward the gate, led them through, then continued to follow the fence until they reached the barn.

Groping in the darkness they unhitched Betsy from the loaded sled, and by touching the barn's wall they were able to lead her to the door without getting lost.

"Oh, it is good to get inside!" Raymond exclaimed when Father lit the lantern. He chuckled when he saw a white horse and noticed how Father and he were covered with snow.

"Good for you, Betsy," Father talked softly to the horse while he rubbed her down. Raymond brought feed and water for her, then went to do the other chores.

The storm was beginning to lessen when they were ready to leave the barn. A feeble light shone from the kitchen window where Mother had placed the lamp to guide them.

"Father's home!" Martha rejoiced when she heard them on the porch. "I knew God would bring them safely home."

Mother returned her oldest daughter's smile. "Yes, God was caring for them." She voiced her own thankfulness at hearing them return.

The Longest Night

Each day the sun lazily peeked over the horizon, chasing away the darkness and turning the earth into dazzling white. For several hours it shone lazily, then disappeared again, leaving the earth wrapped in darkness. Each day it shone less until one day no sunlight shone at all to break the darkness.

"I don't like to have it dark all day," Joanna complained as she placed soup bowls on the table.

"I know, Dear, but we won't have very many dark days. Did you know that there are some people who don't see the sun for a couple of months? So a few days isn't too bad, is it?"

"I guess not," Joanna admitted slowly.

"How would you like to take a walk outside in the twilight? It isn't really as dark as it seems from inside the house."

"Oh, yes, let's!" Joanna brightened. Quickly she finished setting the table, and before long she could hear Father stomping the snow from his boots on the porch.

"Can you guess what Mother and I are going to do after we are finished eating?" Joanna asked at the dinner table, her eyes shining with excitement.

"Um—let me guess. Are you going to wash the dishes?" Father asked teasingly.

"Not that!" Joanna giggled as she took another spoonful of soup. "We're going for a walk in the dark! I can't wait!"

"That does sound interesting," remarked Father as he glanced at Mother. "I can stay inside with Donnie if you want me to," he offered. "It's rather cold outside for him."

After the dishes were put away, Mother and Joanna bundled up ready for their walk. Wide-eyed with excitement, Joanna opened the door for Mother and together they stepped into the frosty, dark day.

How strange everything seemed. No sun shone to dazzle the snow. There was only a quiet darkness everywhere. Joanna looked across the lane toward the sheep barn as it stood forlornly beneath the black outline of the trees. She shivered with an uneasy feeling and slipped a mittened hand into Mother's.

"Let's take the garden path, then walk up the hill behind the barn," Mother suggested. "From there we'll be able to see most of our farm."

No wind was blowing. Stillness reigned everywhere. Even the birds were strangely silent.

"This is so different," Joanna whispered, as though afraid to talk aloud.

The trees along the path cast dark shadows as they stood tall and bare in the twilight. Joanna held onto Mother's hand a little more tightly.

Mother smiled down reassuringly. "It is different, isn't it? Our whole farm seems unfamiliar."

They entered the garden and only the soft crunch of their boots could be heard as they

She shivered with an uneasy feeling and slipped a mittened hand into Mother's.

walked. Ahead they could see the sawmill, dark and quiet. Snow covered the slab piles, making them seem giant and mysterious with dark gaping holes where the snow had not reached.

At the hill's crest, they stopped walking. Below them the barn and house stood shrouded in darkness. Joanna could see the faint glow of lamplight through the windows. Turning, she stared at the dark and foreboding forest behind them.

"Look, Joanna, how quiet the barnyard is. All the animals seem to be sleeping. Maybe they think it is still nighttime." Mother pointed to the barn below them. "I think it is time we get back to the house now. Are you ready?"

"Yes, let's go back," Joanna answered quickly.

"How did you like your walk?" Father asked when they entered the house.

"I'm glad Mother was with me. It's so quiet outside it makes me afraid," Joanna freely admitted as she pulled off her boots. "I think I like it better in the house," she added.

That afternoon as Joanna watched for

the school bus, eager for the school children to come home, she sang softly to herself:

"This little light of mine,
I'm going to let it shine;
This little light of mine,
I'm going to let it shine;
Let it shine,
Let it shine,
Let it shine."

"That's a good song to sing," Mother smiled. "Did you know you can let your light shine even if it is dark all day? When you are happy and obedient, your light is shining."

Joanna nodded, then exclaimed, "I see lights. I see the school bus." She spoke excitedly as she watched the red lights flashing. "Here come Rodney and Martha and Linda and Raymond. Oh, I'm so glad they're home!" Joanna ran to open the door for them.

Joanna sat quietly watching the school children busily eating cookies and drinking milk while they eagerly related what had happened during their day at school.

"Why are you so sober?" Raymond teased when he noticed how quiet Joanna was.

Joanna broke into a smile, then shyly answered, "Mother said that even if it is dark outside all day, I can let my light shine."

"What does Joanna mean?" Rodney asked.

Mother explained. "Joanna was not very happy that the darkness lasted all day long. But then she sang, 'This Little Light of Mine,' and I told her that she could let her light shine by being happy and obedient even though there was darkness outside.

"It does make the day seem brighter," Mother continued, "when you come home from school smiling and eager to tell us your day's experiences." Mother looked fondly at each one. "Our attitudes affect a lot of people. The sun isn't shining and the day has been dark, but how wonderful when we all can be radiating sunshine."

One candle, softly flick'ring,
How welcome is its light;
It gleams and breaks the darkness
Of this enshrouding night.

Warm, glowing, crackling fireplace,
How welcome are its rays,
To drive out cold and dampness—
Bring cheer to dreary days.

Strong, sheltering, home sweet home,
How welcome are your walls,
Your roof above with sturdy beams,
Protects from angry squalls.

Dear precious, loving family,
All gathered here to share,
Our lives with one another;
To help, sustain, and care.

Snowstorm

"It's still snowing!" Martha exclaimed. "Look, Mother, how white it is outdoors!"

Joining Martha at the window, Mother looked in surprise at the whiteness, for all they could see was the swirling, white snow. A gentle snowfall was turning into another raging, northern blizzard. All through the night the snow had fallen softly, covering up the dirty, crusted snow left from the previous storm, and now the world was again wrapped in a thick blanket of pure white fluff.

That morning they had driven to church in the gently falling snowflakes, and on the return trip they had found the road blotted out by the deepening snow. Mother was unprepared for what she now saw through the window. She searched the outdoors for landmarks but could not see them; only the wall of white.

"Father," she spoke with concern. "It's becoming windy. Did you notice?"

"No, I hadn't," he replied. "But if it is blowing, I believe we'll be in for another blizzard." Coming over to stand by Mother, he took in the total whiteness of the outdoors.

"Say, the snow *is* blowing! I think it might be wise to do the chores now," he added with decision. "If this keeps up, we won't make it out to the barn tonight.

"Raymond, Rodney," Father turned to his sons, "let's get dressed for the outdoors and go chore. It's looking bad outside."

After Father and the boys had left for the barn, the house became quiet, for Joanna and Donnie were taking naps. In the heating stove, the fire hissed as a burning log fell, settling lower on the glowing coals. Mother and Martha could hear the wind rising.

"I hate to see anyone go outside,"

Martha frowned to herself as she stared out the window. "What if Father and the boys can't find their way to the barn? Or what if it gets worse before they come in?" She remembered the storm they had before when Father and Raymond were out in the woods.

"Shall we play a game?" Mother's gentle voice broke into Martha's troubled thoughts.

"Yes, let's. I'll get the Bible game," Martha answered eagerly. "Do you want to play, Linda?"

"No, thank you," Linda answered, glancing up from her book.

Soon Mother and Martha were concentrating on the game.

"Do you have Philippians?"

Mother handed a slip of paper to Martha. "Colossians?"

Smiling, Mother handed that paper, too.

Martha was getting excited. All she needed was 1 and 2 Thessalonians and she would have all the New Testament. Should she ask Mother for them, or were they among the few papers still lying in the center of the table?

Martha glanced at Mother, who only answered with a smile.

"Would you have 1 Thessalonians?" she asked slowly. "And 2 Thessalonians?"

Handing 1 Thessalonians to Martha, Mother said, "Sorry, but I'm afraid I don't have 2 Thessalonians."

"Oh, no," Martha groaned inwardly.

It was Mother's turn, and Martha held her breath as she heard her ask.

"Would you happen to have Nahum?"

With relief Martha handed Nahum to Mother. Apparently 2 Thessalonians was still on the table. If only she would get it!

Then it was her turn. "Do you have Malachi?" she asked Mother.

"No, sorry, I don't."

"Good," Martha thought, "maybe I'll get 2 Thessalonians this time." She looked quickly at the paper she had chosen; then disappointed, she placed Malachi with her others.

Each had another turn when in disbelief she heard Mother say, "I'd like Malachi, Matthew, Mark, Luke, John, Acts, Romans, 1 and 2 Corinthians, Galatians, Ephesians, Philippians, Colossians, and 1 Thessalonians."

Martha gathered up the papers and

handed them over.

Then Mother continued, "1 Timothy, 2 Timothy, . . ." until she reached Revelation.

Looking over her remaining papers, Martha noticed that there was only one slip left on the table. What was it? Carefully she went over the books of the Bible that she still had. "Maybe it's Ruth, since I have Judges and 1 Samuel," she reasoned.

"Do you have Ruth, Mother?"

"No, I don't."

"Good!" Martha thought as she took the last slip of paper and saw that it was Ruth.

When her turn came again, she excitedly asked Mother for the Old Testament books she was missing and continued asking until both the Old and New Testaments were complete. She had won the game.

"I have enjoyed playing," Mother said as she closed the book in which she had concealed her slips of paper. "It helps the time to pass more quickly while we're waiting."

"So Mother is concerned, too," Martha thought. She looked at the clock, then back at Mother. "An hour has gone by since they left the house," she commented. "Shouldn't they be finished now?"

"They could soon be here," Mother answered. "But maybe they're doing extra feeding." Then she said softly, "Let's pray for them. It's so easy to become confused when you are trying to find your way in white, swirling snow."

Mother and Martha bowed their heads and Mother prayed. "Heavenly Father, how thankful we are that You are all knowing and can see everything. We ask You to guide Father and the boys that they would be able to find their way in the blinding snow. Thank You for hearing our prayer and answering according to Your will. In Jesus' Name, Amen."

The minutes ticked slowly by in the quiet living room. The soft pelting of snow driven by the wind against the logs of the house was the only answering sound to the clock's steady ticking.

Joining Linda on the couch, Martha picked up a book and tried to read, but her mind kept wandering to the snow-shrouded world.

Bang, bump, bang. The stillness was finally broken by chunks of wood thudding into the woodbox on the enclosed porch.

"Thank You, God, for answering our prayer," Martha breathed in relief.

Then all was quiet again, but this time Martha was able to read her book and enjoy the story, for she knew that Father and the boys were safely at the house.

After awhile the door burst open, bringing in the cold, snow-covered men.

"We're having quite a storm, aren't we?" Mother questioned as she helped sweep snow from coats.

"It's stormy outdoors—a real blizzard. You can't see anything," Father said between breaths. "I'm thankful the chores are done."

"You get a strange feeling when you have no idea where you are," Raymond added. He held his hands over the stove, glad for the warmth.

"I was afraid," Rodney admitted. "Even if I was holding onto Father's or Raymond's hand."

"I don't think that Father was as lost as we were. We followed the barn corrals, then found the chicken house and followed that," Raymond explained. "The open space between the chicken house and our house isn't too long, but it seems miles when you're groping in darkness, not even sure if you're going in the right direction."

Father smiled at Raymond. "What you said is true, but I couldn't tell my directions too well, either. We need to credit God for guiding us, not me. It's really a hopeless feeling when the wind is screaming at you from all directions and you can't see your hand in front of you.

"It is very unusual for our storms to become raging blizzards so quickly. Tomorrow I'm going to fasten a rope to the corner of the chicken house and attach the other end to the house, then if we should ever get caught in a quick storm again, we can safely go to the barn."

"I would be glad if you would do that," Mother agreed wholeheartedly.

How cozy, comfortable, and safe their home seemed that evening. Outside the cold wind was howling, but inside was quiet contentment with all the family gathered around the flickering lamplight.

Snowbound

How peaceful, how quiet, how sparkling and fresh was the world in which the family awoke that Monday morning. But it was, oh, so-o cold!

"B-r-r-r," Raymond shivered as he brought in another armload of wood and dumped it into the woodbox. "It's so icy out on the closed porch it almost freezes your breath. I wonder how cold it is outside."

"Let's find out, Son," Father smiled in answer, "but make sure you wrap up well. A person can get frostbitten without even realizing it when the weather is this bitter."

A wave of frigid air engulfed Father and Raymond as they waded through the drifts to the barn. It seemed hard to breathe as the cold pressed against them, seeping in through their thick layers of clothing.

Raymond swung the barn door shut, grateful for the warmth inside. Climbing the ladder to the hay loft, he was soon busy throwing hay bales down the hay chute. The sweet smell of hay hung in the air, giving the loft a cozy feeling.

Below, Raymond heard the contented movement of the cattle as they noisily munched their feed and hay, the faint clang of a cow bell, and the gentle *maa-maa-a* of the calves as they clambered for attention. Raymond stopped a moment, reveling in the familiar sounds of the barn—even to the faint skitter of the mice he had disturbed. He smiled to himself as he lifted the last bale and effortlessly threw it down the chute. *Thud!* It landed at the bottom with the others.

"I can't imagine what it would be like not to live on a farm," Raymond thought as he lowered himself through the loft hole and down the ladder. "Sure, it's work, sometimes hard work, but I enjoy it," he thought.

When the chores were finished he reached for the pail of milk Father had set by the door. Already the milk had a thin layer of ice around the outside.

Once more the polar air hit them like a sharp, stinging wall. A slight breeze made the cold even more bitter. Driving against their faces it bit and pierced. By the time they made it to the house, the milk was frozen over the top.

"It must be terribly cold outdoors!" Mother exclaimed as she took the milk pails. "Look, the milk is completely frozen over!"

"It is cold. You can hardly bear to be outside," Father answered. Turning to Raymond he continued, "Let's fill the snow barrel and get in some more wood." (A fifty five gallon drum standing behind the stove was a familiar sight in this northland community. Each winter morning and evening it was filled with snow and allowed to melt. The water that accumulated was used for washing dishes, hands, and clothes. It saved carrying water from the well, and snow water was softer water, besides.)

Outside, high, pure-white drifts were everywhere. With one scoop the men had a

Outside, high pure-white drifts were everywhere.

bucket full. Each time they entered the warm house to empty their pails of snow, it seemed colder outside.

Finally they were finished. How snug and warm the house felt as they relaxed in its cozy comfort.

By evening the mercury was as low as it could go on their -50 degree thermometer. Stiff winds blew, howling around the buildings. Iciness penetrated the log house, creeping into every corner and seeping up through the floors.

Merrily the fire crackled until the stove sides glowed red hot, but still the cold was everywhere.

"O Mother, I'm so tired of the cold," Linda complained when the supper dishes were put away. "May we go to school tomorrow?" she pleaded.

"No, Dear, I'm sure there won't be any school as long as it's this cold. It isn't safe for children to be outdoors. Shall we all sing together? We can make popcorn," Mother suggested.

"Yes, let's!" Linda jumped up eagerly, her bored expression gone. "I'll get the songbooks," she offered.

"This is my Father's world,
And to my list'ning ears
All nature sings, and round me rings
The music of the spheres."

The endless beating of the wind was drowned out as joyful voices filled the humble home with praises. Even the cold seemed to retreat a little.

"What does this song declare to us?" Father questioned when they had finished singing.

"That God made the world and everything in it. Even the snow," Rodney answered.

"Yes. And what else does it tell us?" Father looked over at Linda.

Linda caught Father's glance and answered slowly, "I guess that God even made the cold."

"That's right," Father smiled.

"Maybe after we're finished singing, Father can tell us a story about the snow and cold," Mother proposed.

Other songs followed. When the family closed their songbooks sometime later, Linda turned to Father eagerly. "Tell us about the cold, please." Her eyes danced with interest.

"Well, let's see," Father began. "Did you know that when it's very cold, if we didn't have any snow a lot of little animals would die?"

Linda shook her head.

"When it gets cold in the fall, the ground freezes hard like rock. There are little animals that have burrowed holes underground for their homes. Mice, rabbits, and shrews stay awake during the winter, while some animals, like bears, sleep until spring.

"When it snows a couple of feet on top of the frozen ground, it's like laying a thick blanket on the earth. The sun shines down on the snow, melting the top layer which then freezes, forming a crust over the loose, fluffy snow beneath. This crust keeps the snow from blowing away, and the earth keeps its blanket."

Linda listened with interest as Father continued. "When we have a deep snowfall like we did a few days ago, followed by severe cold such as we have now, way down under the snow it is actually nice and warm for the animals. The wind cannot reach them and neither can the bitter cold. See how God is taking care of the animals?"

Linda nodded. "I'm glad," she said.

The smell of popcorn filled the room with its inviting aroma. *Pop, pop, pop, pop.* The kernels danced inside the wire screen popper as Raymond shook it vigorously across the top of the stove.

"I'm glad you told us about the animals," Linda remarked to Father as she reached for a handful of hot popcorn.

"There are always things to learn and to be thankful for," Father remarked. "The snow is our insulator against the cold. Even plants and trees would die without snow for protection."

When the last popcorn kernels had been swept together and dumped into the fire, the family members each took a towel-wrapped, hot brick to their bedrooms. It felt toasty warm against the cold blankets when they crawled into bed.

Sleepily Linda looked up at the frost peeping between the ceiling boards. The smell of popcorn wafted through the house on the cold air. She blew out the lamp, burrowed deeper under the covers, and covered her head to shut out the cold. Before long she was warm and fast asleep.

Winter Wonders

Drip, drip, drip, drip.

Martha stirred restlessly in her sleep.

Drip, drip, drip, drip, drip, drip. The sound persisted.

"What is that?" Martha wondered sleepily as she listened.

Drip, drip, drip, drip.

"Why, it's water dripping!" Martha was wide awake now as she listened to the pleasant sound. "How nice!" she rejoiced. "What a change from being cold, cold, cold."

Quickly Martha got out of bed and soon joined Mother in the kitchen. "Oh, joy!" she announced happily.

> "The snow is melting!
> The sun is shining!
> 'Twill be so pleasant
> With no more whining!"

Mother laughed with her when she finished her rhyme. "Yes, it is pleasant to have warmer weather. The severe cold of the last couple days has made the time seem long for everyone." Then Mother continued seriously, "But we have no reason to complain. The cold days help us to appreciate the nice warm days more, and God wants us to be a thankful people."

A whole week had passed since the last snowstorm and the days of intense cold that followed. Staying indoors all day without school or outdoor chores had made the time seem endless. Today was Saturday, so there was no school again, but this time Martha was glad. It would be good to go outdoors. Quickly she put on her warm, outdoor clothing and left the house to search for Linda and Rodney who had already gone outside.

Martha paused, taking in the beauty of the winter day. The sun dazzled and sparkled on the pure-white snow. Big icicles clung to the roof where snow was still layered thickly. A wind played softly, whistling gently around the buildings and shaking snow from the tree branches. Endless drifts were piled everywhere, blotting out landmarks, small shrubs, and even fences. On and on it stretched, as far as the eye could see, making the buildings and trees seem small as the snow lay piled against them.

Martha was crossing the lane to the sheep barn when Linda opened the kitchen door. "O Mother!" she called breathlessly as she stepped into the house, her rosy cheeks glowing with excitement. "May Rodney and I use Father's snowshoes? In some places we can run on top of the snow, but then, all of a sudden, we fall through."

"I think you may," Mother answered with a smile. "Remember to be careful and to share."

"Oh, we'll share," Linda responded eagerly. "Rodney and I want to go together."

Click. The door latched as Linda hurriedly slipped back outdoors. Entering the dark shop where the snowshoes were kept, Linda stopped, then blinked, trying to see. She waited impatiently for her eyes to adjust to the dimness.

"I have them." Rodney startled her when he spoke.

Linda jumped. "Oh, you scared me," she laughed. "I couldn't see anything after being outdoors. I probably looked funny standing here blinking my eyes," she giggled. "Here, let's take them outside and buckle them on."

The children laid the snowshoes on the snow and Linda soon had her feet buckled fast. "Okay, Rodney, you may stand behind me now. I'm ready."

Rodney stepped onto the snowshoes but was jerked backwards when Linda took the first step. Linda stumbled and fell forward, taking the buckled-on snowshoes with her. Rodney, trying to catch his balance, pitched forward and landed on top of her. Together they fell in a heap on the snow.

"What are you two doing?" Martha exclaimed laughingly.

Linda was sprawled face down in the snow with Rodney across her. The snowshoes stuck out at different angles, nearly as tall as Martha.

Martha helped them up.

Together they fell in a heap in the snow.

"Serves you right for being in such a hurry," Rodney grinned good naturedly.

"It's not that funny," Linda sputtered crossly as she wiped the snow from her face and brushed it from her coat.

"But you should have seen yourself!" Martha chuckled as she remembered the long, gangling snowshoes.

Linda had to smile in spite of herself. "We probably did look silly," she admitted reluctantly. "Look, Martha," she pointed. "We want to walk in the deep snow over by the creek. See how it almost covers the willows in places? Could you help us get started, and do you think the snowshoes will hold us up?"

"They should," Martha answered. "And, yes, I'll help you get started walking."

Rodney stepped on behind Linda again and held onto her coat.

"Don't start walking," Martha told Linda, "until you know Rodney is ready. That's what caused the first spill. I know what. Call out, 'One, two. One, two.' with every step, then Rodney will be able to follow you."

"Ready?" Linda called. "Let's go. One,

two. One, two."

Clumsily, they inched the snowshoes forward.

"One, two. One, two," they slowly moved across the snow.

"Whew! Let's stop," Linda panted after a while. "That's hard work!"

After a little rest they were ready to go again. "One, two. One, two." It was going better.

They were almost to the willows now, and they could tell the snow was not packed as hard. Their snowshoes wanted to sink down into the snow.

"This is fun," Rodney said breathlessly. "Look at the air pockets around the willow branches. How deep would I sink if I stepped off the snowshoes?" he wondered aloud.

"Don't," Linda warned. "I might not be able to pull you out."

They plodded on a little farther, then crossed over the creek to the other side. As they walked away from the creek into the open field, the snow was hard and smooth and the snowshoes seemed to glide along.

"I could walk here, couldn't I?" Rodney asked. Without waiting for an answer, he stepped off onto the snow and gingerly took a couple of steps.

Nothing happened. He took a few more steps. Still nothing happened. The crusty snow held him up.

"I'll race you to the fence," he called back as he ran on top of the hard smooth drift.

The huge drift sloped gently down to meet the next one, creating a small valley between them. Rodney skipped along gaily. Suddenly the snow crust gave away and he dropped down to above his waist in the powdery snow.

He tried to climb out, only to sink a little deeper. Each time he placed his arms on the snow crust around him, it gave way.

"Linda!" he shouted. "Linda! Come help me, I'm stuck!" He floundered helplessly.

Linda cautiously walked close to him, surveying his predicament. "What am I supposed to do?" she puzzled. "These snowshoes are so awkward I can't bend down to help you." She stood thoughtfully trying to think of a way to help Rodney.

"I know," she brightened suddenly. She walked across in front of Rodney to the next drift, which was higher, where she tested the snow. "This drift is rock hard," she informed him. "Now hang onto the snowshoes and I'll pull."

Rodney held on to the snowshoes while Linda strained slowly forward. Rodney was soon able to reach the hardened snow and with an effort pulled himself up, where he sprawled, then crawled a little way before trying to stand up.

"I'm glad I'm out of that trap," he finally breathed with relief. "That was scary!"

Once more Rodney stepped onto the snowshoes behind Linda, and laboriously they made their way toward the house.

"I'm tired," Linda groaned. "These snowshoes are getting so heavy."

Silently they struggled on. "Good, only the fence yet," Rodney announced before long.

Linda perked up. "Then we can take these things off."

Snow completely covered the fence. Only the dark posts stuck up through the snow, to mark the fenceline. At last they were across, leaving the drifts behind.

"I can walk again," she said, as she stepped out of the snowshoes. How light her feet felt!

"Just think," she told Rodney, "when we were walking across the field and beside the creek, I wonder how many little animals we walked over."

"What?" Rodney asked, perplexed. "What do you mean?"

"Remember what Father told us several days ago about little animals being under the snow?"

"Oh, yes, I remember now."

"I guess we'll never know how many animals were under us," a thoughtful Linda said as she picked up the snowshoes. "Let's put these away and go into the house."

The warm kitchen welcomed them with delicious smells. "I'm famished!" Rodney and Linda exclaimed at the same time.

"Take off your wraps," Mother smiled, "and you can each have one cooky. Did you have a nice time on the snowshoes?"

"Yes, we did," they chorused. Between bites of cooky they told Mother all they had done and seen.

"We had so much fun today," Linda sighed contentedly.

"God gave us many things to enjoy,"

Mother said, "and we want always to remember to thank Him for them. He sends the different seasons, and each season is full of many, many wonderful things."

Night Visitors

Linda sat quietly on the living room couch. Spread out before her was a puzzle.

"If only there weren't so many trees, it would make it a lot easier to put together," she sighed.

The house was quiet except for the occasional snapping of the burning wood in the stove. The younger children were already in bed and Linda noticed that Mother had fallen asleep in her chair. Her Bible lay on her lap, almost ready to slide off onto the floor.

Oh, how Linda's throat hurt, and her head felt so dizzy. Thirsty, Linda tiptoed to the kitchen for some water. On her way back she slowly lifted Mother's Bible from her lap and placed it on the stand nearby.

"Guess I'll lie down for a while," she thought. "Time will pass more quickly until the older children and Father come home from church."

Linda reached for a cough drop to ease her burning throat, and then she lay back onto the pillows on the couch. She could hear the wind whistling around the house. The pine trees moaned and swayed. How cozy it was inside the house by the fire. If only she did not have such a miserable cold.

Linda must have dozed, but suddenly she was wide awake. What did she hear? Tensely, she listened. Then she heard the slam of a car door and loud voices.

"Mother," Linda whispered, frightened. "Mother, are you awake?"

"What is it, Dear?" Mother asked sleepily.

"Mother, someone's outside."

By now Mother was wider awake. "Are you sure? Maybe you were dreaming, or maybe it was the wind."

As soon as Mother finished speaking

they heard loud laughter. Quickly Linda got off the couch. "Hear it, Mother?"

"Yes, Dear, I do. Let's go to the kitchen. There is no lamp lit out there. Maybe we can see who it is out the kitchen window."

Mother and Linda entered the dark kitchen and walked over to the window facing the road. It took a moment for their eyes to adjust to the darkness.

"There's a car, Mother," Linda whispered. "It's at the end of our lane."

"Yes, I see it," came Mother's quiet reply.

Together they watched and listened. Before long one of the car doors flew open, and again they could hear loud talk and laughter. While the door was open, the inside car light was on, and they could see five or six men. Suddenly one of the men came sprawling out of the car onto the snow while another jumped out beside him.

Linda was afraid. She watched as Mother went quickly to the door and slipped the bolt into place.

"What can we do?" Linda's words seemed to tumble over each other as she turned to Mother, her eyes wide with fright.

"Come, Dear," came Mother's calm, reassuring answer. "Let's kneel here by the table and ask God to keep us safe."

Together Mother and Linda knelt. Linda's fright slowly left her as she prayed. She realized that God in heaven was watching over them and was aware of the men outside. As they arose from their knees Linda was no longer afraid.

"O Mother," she began, "when I first awoke and heard voices I was frightened. But since we've prayed, I'm not afraid."

"How thankful we can be to know we never need to be afraid," Mother quietly replied. "God is always on the throne." Softly she began singing:

"God is still on the throne, and He will
    remember His own;
Tho' trials may press us and burdens distress
    us, He never will leave us alone;
God is still on the throne, He never forsaketh
    His own;
His promise is true,
He will not forget you,
God is still on the throne."

Everything was still when Mother finished singing. Then once again the stillness was shattered with loud shouting, and they heard the sound of glass breaking. Then, silhouetted against the snow they noticed two figures coming toward the house.

Fear seemed to once more rise in Linda, but she remembered God was watching. "He will take care of us," she thought. "I don't need to be afraid."

As they watched, the men stopped, then turned around and started back to the parked car.

"I think I'll get the lamp," Mother spoke as she went into the living room. Returning, she crossed the kitchen to the outside door and slid the bolt back.

Linda watched, wondering, as Mother opened the door and stepped partially outside, then thrust the lamp up above her head. She held it there for a few moments then softly shut the door.

"What were you doing, Mother?" Linda asked.

"Maybe that will help them leave," Mother answered as she set the lamp on the kitchen table. "Now they know someone is home and that we're not afraid. But come, let's bring your puzzle out here and work on it."

Carefully Mother and Linda carried the puzzle board to the kitchen. Sliding it onto the table, they both stopped as they heard another noise. It was the sound of a car motor. They watched as the car started up the hill and then disappeared.

"Thank You, heavenly Father," Mother whispered. "Let's kneel again, Linda, and thank the Lord for answering our prayer."

Later that night when Father was home from church and had heard of their visitors, he took the lantern and walked out to the end of the lane. He saw the crooked tracks of the two men who had come toward the house. Several beer bottles were lying in the snow. At the end of the lane he found a couple cases of empty bottles and some broken ones.

"How thankful I am your visitors left," Father soberly told Mother when he came back. "By the tracks in the snow they were pushing each other around or falling down. They were drunk, and they would probably not have been easy to cope with if they had chosen to bother you."

As Linda lay in bed that night, she thought of how frightened she had been and of how, after praying and trusting God, the fear had left her. She remembered the song Mother had sung, "God Is Still On the Throne," and how Mother had not been afraid. "I'm so glad my parents have faith in God," she thought as she snuggled deeper under the warm blankets.

Story Time

"Mother, tell me a story, please," Rodney begged as he stood looking out the window into the cold outdoors. This Saturday had seemed so long! He was confined to the house with a cold, so he could not go outside with the older children; the younger ones were sleeping. He watched Mother kneading bread dough at the cupboard. In, out; in, out; her swift hands seemed to fly. He reached for a little scrap of dough lying by itself and popped it into his mouth.

"Could you, Mother?" he asked again.

"I think I could," Mother's eyes

twinkled, "but maybe you could help me first. When I'm ironing, I will tell you a story."

Mother patted the bread dough into a smooth ball before placing it into the pan. She covered the mound of dough with a cloth and set it on top of the stove warmer to rise.

"Now will you please sweep the flour from the floor where I have spilled it while working the bread?" Mother asked.

After Mother wiped the flour from the cupboard, she got the sad irons and placed them on the front part of the stove so they would get hot.

Carefully Rodney swept up the flour. When he had finished, he sat on the couch watching Mother set up the ironing board. Mother checked one of the irons, then moved the other two toward the back of the stove. Hooking the handle onto the hot iron, she carried it to the ironing board, picked up a shirt, and began to iron it.

"Why did you move the other irons back?" Rodney questioned. "Why not let them get real hot so they stay hot longer?"

"Because they will burn the clothes I'm ironing if they are too hot," Mother answered. "You only heat sad irons as hot as you want them to be. By setting them toward the back of the stove, they will stay hot, but they will not get any hotter. When this iron I'm using cools down the others will be the right temperature to use. Shall I tell you a story of when I was a girl just two years older than you are?"

"Yes. Tell me." Rodney's eyes sparkled with anticipation.

"When I was ten years old my parents, or your Grandpa and Grandma, decided to move to another farm five hundred miles away. We didn't own a big truck to move our things, neither did Grandpa have enough money to pay what it would have cost to hire someone.

"So Grandpa decided to fix up our wagons and use them. The first wagon held pigs, chickens, and some feed for them—also some grain for the horses that pulled the wagons.

"The second wagon carried still more feed and some furniture. Our third wagon was named the "junk wagon" because it carried a little bit of everything. Last was the fourth wagon, which was to be our home.

"In the back part of our wagon-home were our beds with curtains between them for bedrooms. In the front part, along the sides, were a cupboard, wash sink, sewing machine, and woodbox. Our wood cookstove stood in the center of the front section with a cream separator beside it. A big tent covered the wagon, making it nice and cozy. Grandpa mounted a ladder on the wagon's side so we could easily climb up into the wagon or down from it.

"Grandma always drove the house wagon, sitting on the edge of the cookstove to hold the horses' reins. My oldest brother, your Uncle Jonathan, rode a saddle pony so he could herd the cows which grazed along the roadside as we traveled.

"It was springtime when we began traveling. Often the dirt roads would be muddy from rains. There would, sometimes, be big mud holes in which a wagon would get stuck. Then Grandpa would have to unhitch a pair of horses from another wagon and hitch them in front of the pair of horses that was pulling the wagon that was stuck. The two teams would be able to pull the wagon out. Sometimes each wagon would have to

The two teams would be able to pull the wagon out.

be pulled through in this way.

"Every evening we stopped and camped. Sometimes at a farmhouse, sometimes in a schoolyard, and sometimes just along the road. Each day the chickens, pigs, cows, and horses had to be fed and cared for. After the cows were milked, Grandma would separate the milk, saving the cream in cream cans to sell at the next town we passed through. Each morning we would get up early to do the chores again.

"Whenever Grandma needed to bake bread, she would work the bread dough the evening before and let it rise all night so it would be ready to bake early the next morning. Sometimes we would camp all day so Grandma could wash clothes and clean our little home on wheels.

"At first it was great fun traveling in our wagonhome, but after a while we got weary of it. On poor traveling days we covered only ten or fifteen miles. On good days we would go perhaps twenty or twenty-five miles.

"Sometimes a wagon wheel would come off and we would have to stop and wait until Grandpa fixed it. Then there were times when the mosquitoes were so thick we thought we would be eaten alive. There were days when it was chilly and rainy, and other days when it became unbearably hot. On the hot days, we would stop and rest for several hours at noon before traveling again.

"One day Grandma was climbing down the ladder when her dress caught, causing her to fall and hurt her arm, leg, and head. I remember Grandma and Grandpa thanking God because Grandma was not hurt any worse."

Mother thoughtfully hung up a dress before continuing. "Another time we were traveling through a section of hilly country. It was very windy that day and the wind was blowing big balls of tumbleweeds and thistles. How funny it looked to see these balls roll over and over, racing as if they were trying to catch each other.

"Day after day, week after week we traveled for a little over five weeks until we arrived at our new home." The story was done and the ironing was finished. Quietly Mother put the irons back into the stove warmer.

Rodney watched, thinking of the wagon-home Mother had lived in for so many weeks.

He liked their own cozy kitchen and was glad they did not need to travel day after day.

"Thank you for the story, Mother," he said as Mother folded the ironing board. "I'm glad for our home."

"I am, too," Mother smiled as she came and sat beside Rodney. "I'm sure Grandma and Grandpa were glad to arrive at their new home. It took a long time to get there, but even though we were traveling and away from home, God was with us. All the time, God kept us safe. I remember being so glad to finally live in a house that wasn't moving."

There was a smile of contentment on Mother's face as she got up to begin the next task.

Across the Ice

"Br-r-r-r, it's another cold day," Father announced as he quickly shut the door.

"Does that mean we won't be able to visit Grandma Millers today?" Rodney asked. He had been waiting and waiting for this day to come. It was not often that the weather moderated sufficiently for them to go visiting in the wintertime, so this was something special.

"No, it is not too cold to go," Father smiled at Rodney's eagerness. "Does that make you happy?"

"Oh, yes, yes." Rodney's eyes sparkled

with excitement.

Mother looked up from the stove where she was stirring the oatmeal, and asked, "How cold is it this morning?"

"Twenty degrees below, but there is no wind, so the horses should be able to stand the drive," Father replied as he took his place at the table.

Talking excitedly about the day ahead, the children pulled out their chairs and sat down for breakfast. Everyone became silent as Father reached for the Bible. As he read, he paused occasionally and explained in simple words what he had read so everyone would understand. Then, as the family knelt beside their chairs, Father prayed, asking God to guide them through the day and to keep them from the evils and dangers they might face.

With breakfast over, everyone hurriedly went about their morning work. Then winter coats, boots, mitts, scarves, and blankets were located, and everyone prepared for the cold drive ahead.

"I'm so excited I can hardly get dressed," Joanna giggled. Hurriedly, she pulled on a mitten, only to find it was on the wrong hand.

"O Martha," she wailed, "please, help me. I just can't get dressed right."

Martha smiled and came to see what the problem was. "Let's start over again and maybe this time things will go right." She gave the mitten a final tug, then whispered, "I'm excited, too!"

Everyone was finally ready. The family left the warmth of the house and hurried to the waiting sleigh. Stopping, Linda watched in fascination as the horses snorted and tossed their heads, sending their breath in white-cloud puffs. They pawed impatiently. It seemed as if they were as excited about going visiting as was everyone else.

Linda was the last one to take her place on the benches which ran along the sides of the sleigh. How nice and cozy the sleigh was. Linda gave a contented sigh in anticipation of the fun of flying for miles across the snow.

The sleigh was homemade and was like a miniature house. It had a roof, sides, windows, and a door. There was a small wood stove in the middle of the sleigh which kept them warm. The door had a window through which Father put the reins. He could drive the horses from inside the warm sleigh.

"I believe we will take the lake route," Father announced as he started the horses and headed them toward the barn. "Though last week was warmer, we've had a couple days of colder weather since, and the lake should be frozen good. Spring is on the way and we won't be able to drive the sleigh over the lake much longer." Crossing the lake cut the distance to Grandma's house in half. It was eight miles by the rough and rutty road.

Swinging around the corner of the barn, the horses started climbing the hill. Heading across the open field at the hill's crest, they broke into a gentle trot, then slowly descended the gentle slope toward the lake. Snow spraying out from the sides of the runners made a gentle hissing sound.

Crowding close to Father, Linda peered out the front window. Sunlight dazzled the snow, making it so bright it hurt her eyes, yet she wanted to keep watching. She wanted to see the trees, tall and silent as they surrounded the lake, their branches loaded down with snow. She wanted to see the snowshoe rabbits as they jumped up and ran when the horses came too close. It was fun to watch them zigzag to safety.

Soon Father pulled gently on the reins, slowing the horses as they started across the ice. The lake looked smooth and strong and stretched before them in its whiteness. They could hear the hum of the sleigh runners and the hollow clop, clop of the horses' hooves as they trotted across the ice.

Suddenly the sleigh seemed to lurch and they felt as though they were swaying and tipping.

"The ice!" Father gasped. He had hardly uttered the words when *crack, crack, crack,*

Behind them dark water oozed out of the broken ice.

they could hear the ice breaking. As Father yelled, "Giddap", and frantically slapped the reins, one of the horses stumbled and broke through the ice.

Straining every muscle, the other horse gave a terrific lunge, jerking the fallen horse back up on solid ice. The fallen horse regained his footing and together both horses surged forward, bringing the tipping sleigh across the broken ice. The horses kept running, and in a few frenzied moments they reached the shore and solid ground. Behind them dark water oozed out of the broken ice and spread, blotting out the whiteness of the snow.

Everything had happened so quickly the shaken family sat stunned and silent. Then Mother spoke with deep feeling. "Praise God for protecting us."

"Yes," Father agreed fervently. "Only God's guardian angel kept our horses and small sleigh from going down into the lake when the ice broke."

Father stopped the horses. Climbing out, he checked to see if the horse which had broken through the ice was all right.

"I'll need a blanket to rub the horse's legs," Father stated to Mother as he opened the door. "Otherwise, I believe he's all right."

When Father had finished rubbing down the horse, he climbed into the sleigh and said to the family, "Let's bow our heads and thank our heavenly Father for keeping us safe." Then Father prayed, "We thank Thee, dear Lord, for sparing us from danger and for Thy promises in Thy Word which we can claim. For Thy Word says, 'The angel of the Lord encampeth round about them that fear him, and delivereth them.' We thank Thee for this deliverance and may it help each one of us to put our trust more fully in Thee. In Jesus' Name. Amen."

Once again they started on their way. This time they moved more slowly as the horses climbed the slight hill above the lake. After winding through evergreen trees, they came out onto level ground. Just ahead was their log church house flanked by stables in which they kept their horses during the worship service. Silently they drove through the church yard and onto the road which led to the Millers.

"Well, that's the last trip across the lake for this year," remarked Father, breaking the silence. "I surely prefer to travel that route.

It's always so pretty and quiet and easy."

"Remember all the rabbits and birds we saw?" Joanna asked.

"And remember that moose we saw standing so still?" added Rodney.

"Yes. God has given us a beautiful world to enjoy. Let's sing 'This Is My Father's World,' " suggested Father.

As the family drove the last remaining miles, the sleigh was filled with joyful voices lifted in thanksgiving and praise.

"Could we sing, 'God Will Take Care of You'," Martha asked as they rounded the last corner and Grandma Miller's house came into view.

Once again the little sleigh was filled with praises as they sang,

"God will take care of you,
Through ev'ry day,
O'er all the way;
He will take care of you,
God will take care of you."

Stealthily, silent, and wary,
They pad through the deepening night;
Stopping and sniffing alertly,
Before hast'ning on in their flight.
Circling to measure the distance,
Then striking with speed and with might;
Greedily devouring their prey,
Then fleeing, ere daybreak brings light.

Spring Prowler

Spring was showing its face. Snow was slowly melting, soaking into the earth and running in tiny streams toward the creek. There it met swift-flowing waters strewn with ice, branches, and large cakes of snow the waters had grabbed from unsuspecting snowbanks flanking its sides. The sun shone warmer, brighter, and longer, awakening the earth from its sleep.

Spring, spring is here! the wind whispered softly as it blew gently to help the snow and water disappear so new life could come from the earth. Tiny white flowers were struggling through the snow, wanting to catch a glimpse of warm sunlight. *Hurry,* they seemed to say in their eagerness, *we've been sleeping long enough.*

Even the animals knew it was time to awaken from their winter sleep. Squirrels could be seen scurrying up and down the trees as they tidied up their homes. The robin had found its way back from the southland and was busy preparing its nest. Animals left tracks here and there in their search for food. Small tracks, middle-sized ones, and even the huge footprints of bear could be seen in the soft earth.

"One of our spring prowlers is back again," Father stated one morning when he came in from chores.

"What prowler?" Rodney asked, puzzled.

"They're soft, furry, and big," Father answered. "Almost as tall as I am. Can you guess what prowler I'm talking about?" he asked teasingly.

"Bear?" Rodney guessed.

"Yes, the bears are awake and looking for food."

"Bears?" Joanna whispered, wide-eyed. "Great big black bears are around our place?''

"I believe they are, but you need not be afraid," Father reassured her.

"Only one came around the sheep corrals last night. This time of the year they are extremely hungry from sleeping through the winter without food. The bear probably smelled our sheep and could hear them bleating in the barn which made him come so close to our buildings," Father explained.

The next morning Raymond drove the tractor and the stoneboat with the empty water barrels to the pump behind the sheep barn. Steadily he pumped the handle up and down, up and down, watching the water gush into the first big barrel. A damp, musty odor drifted up from the freshly pumped water.

"I wonder how old this well is," he mused to himself as he looked at the frost-covered floor boards. How he hated the wet, slimy boards and the swampy smell. He did not mind pumping water now, though, when snow or frost covered the mossy boards and cancelled out the mucky smell.

Splash, splash. Raymond quickly awoke from daydreaming as he heard the water spill over the top of the full barrel. Jumping down from the pump's platform he slowly moved the tractor ahead until the second barrel was under the pump's spout. Quickly he pumped that one full.

He was now ready to take the water to the sheep barn. Carefully he eased the little tractor forward but still some water slopped onto the wooden platform of the low stoneboat as its wooden runners slid across the ground.

When Raymond came along side the sheep barn he let out a loud whistle. Huge bear tracks were everywhere! As Raymond, in his excitement, allowed the tractor to lurch to a quick stop, water splashed everywhere.

"Oh, no," Raymond groaned as he watched the precious water run onto the ground. "Now I'll probably have to get more! Father," he called, "did you know the bear was back again?"

"I'm not surprised," Father replied. "I hope he won't bother us too much. Let's go have a look at his tracks. We may have to build a bear trap yet."

When chores were finished Raymond hurried to the house to tell Mother what they had seen. "I can't imagine how the bear got on the sheep barn roof!'' he exclaimed when he finished. "The tracks are real plain there because they are muddy tracks. Father says we'll have to make a trap before he does some damage.''

Rodney listened quietly as Raymond talked to Mother. It made him shiver to think that a bear—a real, live, huge, fierce bear—had been just across the road last night—and had even climbed up onto the low sheep barn roof! "I wonder what he'll do next?'' he thought.

After breakfast Father, Raymond, and Rodney checked the bear tracks around the sheep barn more carefully.

"Raymond, Rodney come here,'' Father called.

Raymond and Rodney hurried over to where Father was examining a tree. Bark had been stripped, showing the white, smooth wood underneath.

"Look at the claw marks,'' Father said, showing them the rough gouges made by the bear's sharp claws. "This bear is a couple of years old, I believe. And he must be extremely hungry.''

Looking farther into the forest behind the

sheep barn, they could clearly see from what direction the bear had come. They could even see the old tracks from the night before.

"His den must be in that direction, past this pine grove," Father pointed. "I believe this grove of pines would be a good place to set a trap."

Soon the forest vibrated with the shrill scream of the chain saw.

Crash! Thud! A small tree fell to the ground.

Chop, chop. Raymond swung his axe, cutting off tree branches.

Crash! Thud! Another tree hit the ground.

As the morning progressed, the pile of limbed logs grew.

"I believe we have enough logs now," Father called when there was a lull in Raymond's chopping. "Finish limbing these trees while I get the trap and bait."

"What are you going to use for bait?" Raymond asked.

"The pig that died the other morning should work well," Father replied.

Father and Rodney left, and Raymond hurried to finish limbing the trees. "I hope

I can finish before Father comes," he thought. "I'd surely like to look around some more."

Chop, chop, chop—Raymond's axe cleanly sliced away the small branches. He was working on his last tree when he heard the whine of the approaching tractor.

"Oh, well," he thought resignedly, "maybe I'll have time later on."

Father showed Raymond how to join the limbed logs between the dense pine branches. The lowest branches touched the ground, making it easy to place the logs so they would form two walls. The two sturdy walls were angled so when the trap was finished, it formed a *V*. The outside logs were hidden by the evergreen branches and were hardly noticeable. Father then cut away the branches and brush that were inside the long, narrow trap.

Father dragged the dead pig to the inside tip of the *V*. He securely staked a steel bear trap just inside the entrance, and he set it. Rodney helped Father cover the trap with branches. He had no desire to get close to the sharp steel claws.

The open end of the hidden, wedge-shaped structure was narrow, and the only way the bear could reach the pig was to go over the trap. Everything was ready. All they could do was wait.

"Do you want to scout around with me?" Raymond invited Rodney as Father gathered the tools together and prepared to leave.

"Yes! Let's!" Rodney readily agreed.

As the boys followed the bear's tracks deeper into the woods, they were disappointed to find nothing of significance—only broken underbrush and a few trees with stripped bark. Before long they returned to the house.

Morning finally came. As soon as it was light enough to see, Raymond and Rodney were up and eager to go with Father to check the steel trap. Impatiently they waited while Father checked and loaded his gun.

"Rodney, I want you to stay by the sheep barn," Father instructed kindly. "I'll call when it's safe to come."

In disappointment, Rodney watched as Father and Raymond disappeared among the trees. Slowly the minutes ticked by. The twittering of a bird broke the morning silence. Rodney could hear the faint bleating of the lambs inside the sheep barn.

What was happening? Where were Father and Raymond? Was the bear caught? Did the trap hold it or did the bear manage to break loose? Many questions raced through Rodney's mind as he anxiously waited.

Crack! Rodney jumped at the sound of the gun. "We must have caught him!" he breathed excitedly. Would Father never call? Restlessly he waited. He knew it was safest not to be in a hurry. A person never knew what a bear would do next—even one you thought was dead.

"Ya-ho!"

Rodney needed no second call. Like a shot he was off, running toward Father.

Breathlessly, he arrived at the trap. There lay a huge black bear just inside the entrance. As Rodney panted into sight, Father and Raymond were examining the massive beast. How strong and rugged it had been. Raymond felt regrets that the magnificent animal was dead.

Later that morning, Father and the boys pulled the bear out of the trap with the tractor and loaded it onto the stoneboat.

Father hung the bear from the tripod.

Slowly they moved across the road and up the lane. They stopped at the back of the house where a tripod was waiting. Mother and the rest of the children came out to see the huge furry carcass.

"How old do you think it is?" Raymond asked as Father checked the bear's teeth.

"Around three years old, as close as I can figure," Father answered. "My, but this bearskin will make a nice rug. Come, Dear, and feel this fur," Father encouraged Joanna who was peeping out from behind Mother's skirt.

Cautiously Joanna touched the black hair. "It's really soft!" she said in surprise.

"Yes, it is," Father answered. "It's thick and silky. Won't that make a nice rug to walk on next winter?"

Joanna nodded her head in agreement, as she stroked the thick, black fur again.

Excitedly the children watched as Father hoisted the bear, hung it from the tripod, and began skinning it.

"How will you make a rug out of that?" Linda wondered as she watched Father spread the hide on the ground.

"We will soak it in a salt solution for a

few days. Then when it is cured, I'll let it dry," Father explained. He scraped the inside, fatty layer of the bear hide. "After it is dry, I'll need to make the hide flexible by rubbing it and stretching it with my hands."

"I'm so thankful we were able to get a bear," Mother remarked when Father had finished explaining about the rug. "Bear sausage will taste good for a change."

"And I can't wait until I can walk on the soft rug," Joanna added, once again running her fingers through the fur's thickness. She glanced at Father, and Father's eyes twinkled back at her.

Wagon Car

"Our truck can't be fixed," Father informed Mother one evening. "I guess it's just completely worn out." For several days he had been working on the engine trying to get it to run again, but he had not had any success.

"What do we do now?" Mother questioned.

"The only thing I know to do is use the tractor and wagon this spring and summer. Maybe after harvest we will be able to afford another vehicle. God knows our need and can supply it; until He provides another vehicle, we will do without."

"That won't be bad," Mother replied cheerfully. "Spring is here and the days will keep getting warmer."

Several weeks passed, and twice all the family but Father and Raymond missed church because of bad weather. Brother Waynes, the only family living near enough to offer help, had gladly stopped by to pick up Father and Raymond in their small Ford car, but they did not have enough room for the whole family. Mother had a Bible study with the children at home on those Sundays. Once more it was Sunday, and this time the day had dawned bright and clear.

"O welcome Sunday morning,
     A gift from God above;
It comes with heaven's warning,
     It comes with heaven's love."

Sleepily Martha opened her eyes, then rolled over again, listening to Mother's soft voice drifting through the house.

"The day comes back again,
     The gift of God to men,
The day when Jesus rose
     Triumphant o'er His foes."

"How nice to be awakened with singing,"

she thought. She quietly slipped out of bed so she would not awaken Joanna. Glancing over at Linda, Martha noticed that she, too, was sleeping. "Linda, Linda," she called softly, "it's Sunday morning, so you had better wake up." Gently she shook her younger sister.

Linda yawned; then suddenly she was wide-awake. "Oh, good, it's Sunday!" she whispered excitedly. Hurriedly she tiptoed over to the window and raised the blind, letting the bright morning sunlight flood the bedroom. She noticed the deep blue sky with only a few clouds lazily drifting by. What a lovely morning! She looked toward the barn. The cows were leaving and she could hear the *tinkle, tinkle* of their bells as they followed the cow path along the fence. She watched until the first cow climbed the small hill and disappeared.

"Such a perfect morning!" she whispered aloud as she turned away from the window and looked at Martha. "I was hoping it wouldn't be rainy or cloudy today. Since our poor old truck refuses to run any more, I'm glad for a nice day when we can all go to church."

"Yes, it is beautiful, but we'd better hurry so we can help Mother," Martha replied as she reached for an apron. Inwardly she sighed. Why did they have to use the tractor and wagon? Why couldn't they afford a vehicle like others could? "But at least we are all able to go to church again," she thought resignedly as she left the room. She should be thankful for that.

Linda did hurry and soon she, too, was ready to put on an apron over her Sunday dress.

"Good morning, Linda," Mother smiled cheerfully to her daughter as she entered the kitchen. "Did you notice the beautiful Lord's Day God has given to us?"

"Oh, yes, Mother." Linda's eyes sparkled. "The first thing I did when I got up, was to go to the window to see if it was a nice day! And I'm so glad it is."

"We all are," Mother answered softly. "It's hard to have to stay at home on Sunday. But God has given us a sunny Sunday today."

Slowly Mother stirred the kettle of hot chocolate. "You may set the table, Linda, while Martha gets the younger children up and dressed," she directed. "Father, Raymond, and Rodney will soon be in for breakfast."

Linda counted eight cups, and setting them on the table, she went back to the cupboard for the knives and spoons. Setting the table for Sunday morning breakfast was always fun. Just cups and silverware to set on. They always had hot chocolate and bread for Sunday breakfast, a treat they all enjoyed.

As Linda carried the plate of sliced homemade bread to the table, she heard the door bang shut. Father and the boys were in from doing chores. Before long they were all seated at the table, and once again Mother started singing their Sunday song, " 'O Welcome Sunday Morning.' " Then Father's deep bass voice led out as together they prayed the Lord's Prayer. Even little Donnie could repeat parts of the prayer from memory.

While Mother filled each cup with steaming hot chocolate, Linda cut her buttered bread in strips. She loved to dip her bread into the steaming chocolate just enough to melt the butter a little. "Um-m, this is good," she remarked after taking her first bite.

"I wish we had hot chocolate with bread for breakfast more often," Joanna sighed wistfully as she waited for Martha to spread her second piece of bread.

"Then you wouldn't think it was such a treat and would get tired of it," Father smiled kindly. "It does taste good, though," he agreed, "especially considering the five-mile ride ahead of us. The sun is shining, and the day will warm up, but the air is still chilly at this time of the morning."

As soon as breakfast was over, Raymond slipped into his jacket and cap and called to Martha. "Tell Father I'm bringing the tractor and wagon up to the house."

As he walked from the house, Raymond's thoughts turned to what he had overheard Father telling Mother. "We desperately need another vehicle," Father had said, "but we have no means with which to purchase one. We will just need to trust and let God supply our need."

Raymond breathed deeply of the fresh morning air. He was old enough to realize the blessing it was when everyone was able to go to church.

Martha was waiting with an armload of blankets when he pulled up to the house with the tractor.

"I'll help you," Raymond offered, jumping off the tractor.

Together they spread the blankets along the sides of the hay wagon.

"Ready?" he asked, lifting Joanna up onto a blanket.

"And you?" Raymond grinned as he gave Rodney a helping hand. Raymond took his place on the tractor seat and waited until the rest of the family were seated. Mother and Martha helped the younger children tuck the blankets around their laps and legs.

"Everyone set?" Raymond called. He put the little Ford tractor into gear and eased out the clutch, slowly starting the tractor without a jerk. They soon turned onto the road, and the little tractor picked up speed. Little Donnie snuggled closer to Father, smiling his enjoyment of their open-air vehicle.

"Look, Martha, see those little white flowers?" Linda pointed to the fence which bordered the forest and road. "What are they, Father?"

"Those are called galanthers, or "snowdrops." They're the first spring flower to come up. Sometimes I've seen them blooming when there was still a little snow left on the ground," Father informed her.

"Everyone hang on," Father instructed as they started down the hill. Below, they could see where the road forked. Raymond slowed down, taking the sharp curve to the right. The wagon bumped and jolted as they left the gravel road and started on the more narrow dirt road. It was still muddy from the thawing frost, and soon the tractor wheels were slinging bits of mud into the air. Some came close to landing on them.

"I surely hope we don't have to pass a car," Martha thought grimly. She remembered her struggle several weeks ago when she had first heard they would have to use the tractor and wagon. "I guess Mother was right when she called it pride," Martha admitted.

Up ahead she saw Faye Block's house. The dreary, gray, weather-beaten house was surrounded with bits and pieces of discarded junk. She watched as Faye left the house and

picked her way across the yard to the road.
Martha waved, then moved over to make
room for Faye to sit between herself and
Linda.

"Hello," Faye shyly responded to Mother
and Father's greetings. Faye said very little,
but she was always ready and waiting when
they stopped for her on their way to church.

Laboriously the little tractor climbed the

*They climbed down
from the parked wagon.*

105

last long hill. It was colder as they drove between the dark evergreens that bordered both sides of the road. When they reached the top and had left the forest behind, they could see the church house ahead. The sight of the small white log church nestled among the trees always seemed to warm them.

It's good to stand again!" Mother commented as she climbed down from the parked wagon and began to fold the blankets. "We made good time though," she added. "It took us only about a half-hour."

Inside the quiet church the warm stove beckoned invitingly to them. How good it felt! A few minutes passed; then they heard the crunch of gravel as the first car arrived.

"Children, it's time to hang up your coats and take your places." Father spoke quietly as he helped Donnie unbutton his coat.

"God bless you, Brother John," greeted Brother Wayne as he entered the church. "We are thankful the whole family could come again." He smiled as he shook hands with each one. "God has surely blessed us with a beautiful Lord's Day."

"Yes, and for it we are truly grateful," Father added sincerely.

Kindness

"Let's go sit down," Martha whispered to Faye, and Faye quietly followed her to one of the front benches. Martha glanced over at the clock. "About ten minutes until starting time." Then she noticed the attendance board. "Only twenty-eight people were here last Sunday. I wonder who was missing besides us?" She recalled the cold wind that had kept them at home.

Cr-unch, cr-unch. Another car was driving into the graveled church yard. The minutes ticked slowly by as they waited for others to arrive. The long windowpanes rattled as the church door opened and closed.

Martha looked outside into the quiet, gray forest nearby. How she loved their little log church house, which formerly had been a one-room country school.

She awoke from her daydreaming when Dorothy slipped in beside her. Returning Dorothy's smile, she gave her friend's hand a quick squeeze. It seemed ages since she had talked with Dorothy. How nice it was to see her again! Her attention was turned to their minister, Brother Wayne, as he rose to speak.

"How grateful we each should be for the privilege of coming together in this way to worship our Lord and risen Savior. I'm especially thankful to see that most of the families in our congregation are able to be here this morning. May God be in our midst and bless His Word."

Brother Edwin came forward and announced the opening song. The little church rang with praises as the congregation sang the familiar words of the hymn "*Near to the Heart of God.*"

Martha noticed Faye's eager attention as she drank in the words of the hymn. What would it be like never to have been taught about God? Martha felt ashamed that she had ever wished to stay at home instead of riding to church on the wagon. With thanksgiving she sang the words, "A place where all is joy and peace, / Near to the heart of God."

Swiftly the morning passed as they feasted on and fellowshiped around the Word of God. After the last hymn was sung and church was dismissed, Martha turned to see if all the families were present. Jim Millers, Martins, Wilford's family, the Earl boys, Brother Waynes, David and his mother, and Dorothy's parents were there.

"Where's Grandma Miller?" Martha questioned Dorothy.

"She wasn't here last Sunday, either," Dorothy informed her. "Mother said she fell and hasn't been feeling well since. With no services here tonight, we want to come back after the chores are finished and visit her."

A plan began forming in Martha's mind. "Maybe Dorothy could come to our house for dinner and when her folks come back in the evening, they could get her. But then, likely, she won't want to ride with us in the wagon," Martha thought with a sinking feeling.

"What are you thinking?" Dorothy questioned as a slight frown appeared on Martha's face.

"Oh," Martha laughed softly. "I was thinking up some big plans." Hesitantly she continued. "Would you want to come home with me if your parents could get you this evening? That is if it suits our mothers."

The girls found their mothers talking together, and presented the plan for their approval.

"If you are coming back in the evening," Martha's mother reflected, "maybe your whole family could come for supper before going to visit Grandma Miller. I'm sure it will suit John all right."

"We would enjoy coming," Dorothy's mother answered with a smile. "I'll talk to Harold and see what he says."

A few minutes later she brought an answer. "It will suit, only please don't make a big supper. Just a very light lunch is sufficient for us."

With a smile of happy anticipation Martha and Dorothy settled themselves in the wagon. Homeward the tractor sped, bouncing over the rutty mud tracks.

"You are fortunate to be able to come to church on a wagon," Dorothy commented.

Martha looked at her, hardly believing her ears. "What did you say?"

"I said you are fortunate you can use a wagon instead of a car; this is a lot more fun."

Martha was silent for a few minutes, then slowly she confessed to her friend, "I was afraid to invite you for fear you wouldn't want to ride like this."

"O Martha," Dorothy laughed. "I've been waiting and waiting for a chance. I even wished we could come on a wagon, but fifteen miles would be a rather long ride."

The day passed quickly for the friends. All too soon supper was over and Dorothy's family was saying "good-by."

Martha overheard Sister Joyce tell Mother, "We will plan for you to come on Sunday unless we get a letter. It's been a long time since your family came out our way."

"Lord willing, we will come," Mother answered.

"Are we invited to their place?" Martha questioned Mother when Dorothy's family had left.

"Yes. Next Sunday is Easter Sunday and they would like our family to come for dinner."

"But how will we get over there? Surely not with the tractor and wagon!"

"Dorothy's grandparents from Oregon are going to be at Brother Harolds over Easter. They have a car, and we can go with them," Mother explained. "Brother Harolds want us to stay for the day, and the grandparents will bring us home after the evening services."

"Isn't that kind of them!" Martha exclaimed.

"Yes, it is," Mother answered softly. "They are very dear friends—always helping others."

"A friend loveth at all times" (Proverbs 17:17).

"Be ye kind one to another" (Ephesians 4:32).

Pride

Swish. Bang. The school bus door shut behind the children. Running up the lane toward the house, Linda and Rodney dodged one mud puddle, then skipped over the next one. Raymond and Martha walked slowly behind, sharing the events of the day.

"Mother, we're home!" Rodney and Linda called breathlessly as they burst through the door.

"I'm in the bedroom," came Mother's quiet call.

Joanna's face peered around the door, smiling mischievously. She watched as Linda pulled off her boots and hung up her coat. "Mother's going to do something special for you," she informed Linda knowingly.

"For me!" Linda asked. She followed Joanna as she skipped into Mother's bedroom.

Dresses were spread out on the bed, and Mother was busily digging through a box.

"Hello, Dear," Mother greeted. "Did you have a good school day?"

At the thought of school, the brightness faded from Linda's face. "I guess," she replied with little enthusiasm. "As good as can be expected with no one from our church to be a close friend with."

Mother's heart ached as she looked into her daughter's downcast face. How she wished their children would not have to attend a public school. Maybe someday things would be different. They were hoping and praying so.

"What are you doing with these clothes?" Linda asked, breaking into Mother's thoughts with a change of subject.

"Aunt Barbara sent them. How would you like a new dress?"

"A new dress! Oh, will you make me

one?" Linda's eyes sparkled.

"Most of these clothes are like new," Mother answered as she picked up a pale green dress with white dots. "I thought I'd cut this one down to fit you."

"I would like that," Linda assented happily. She held the dress up to herself, trying to imagine what it would be like. Looking down at the long dress that reached the floor, Linda noticed that the sleeves almost reached to the hem of her dress.

"Mother," she questioned, "could I have long sleeves? Right to my wrists?"

Mother looked at the dress, then at Linda. Thoughtfully she answered, "Wouldn't they get in your way when you wash dishes—or be too warm this summer?"

"Oh, no," Linda responded quickly. "I could push them up, and besides, it's still cool outside, so I won't get too hot."

"Well, I suppose," Mother reluctantly agreed. "But summer will soon be here, and you will want to wear it then, too."

"I'll wear it," Linda answered eagerly. "I don't think I'll get too warm."

"Well, go change your school clothes now," Mother told her.

The next day after getting off the school bus, Linda once more raced for the house.

"Are you finished with my dress?" Her words tumbled over each other in her eagerness.

"Yes," Mother answered. "You may try it on."

Tingling with excitement, Linda slipped into the new dress. How soft and smooth the sleeves felt. Slowly she raised her arms, admiring the long sleeves. "It makes me feel so much older," she thought with a smile of satisfaction.

Pleased, Linda once more turned to examine herself, but was startled when she heard Mother's voice. "It fits you nicely, Linda. Hang it up in the closet and get into an everyday dress now."

"How long was Mother watching?" Linda wondered uneasily when she saw the sober look on Mother's face. Quickly she hung up the dress, but could not resist giving it one more admiring look.

The dress was not mentioned again, but Linda often thought about it and longed for Sunday to come. Whenever she had to get something from the closet, Linda fingered her dress, remembering how nice the long sleeves had looked.

At last it was Sunday. Linda did not need to be reminded to hurry and help with the dishes. She was eager to get finished so she could go and dress for church.

"I believe the sleeves look nicer even than I remembered they did," she thought as she smoothed them with satisfaction. "I'm glad we're going to church in a car this morning." Somehow it seemed important not to ride on the tractor and wagon.

"Don't you think you should take another dress along, or an apron?" Mother questioned Linda as they waited for Harolds to pick them up.

"Martha doesn't," Linda quickly pleaded. "I'll be careful."

Mother remained silent for a moment. The same thoughtful expression appeared on her face that Linda had seen before. "You may go without an apron this time," Mother told her quietly.

Linda was relieved. But why did Mother have to look like that? She pushed the troubling thoughts away and hurried out to the waiting car.

Linda sat down very carefully in church and folded her hands in her lap. She tried to keep her mind on the sermon, but every so often her eyes would wander to her lap where her hands lay. The long sleeves came down so nicely with only her hands showing. Inwardly she sighed, hoping church would soon be over. Brother Wayne seemed to be preaching so long today.

"I wonder if Anna will notice?" were Linda's next thoughts. She glanced at her folded hands again.

When the church service was finally over, Linda stood quietly beside Mother as Mother visited with the sisters. Anna came over to Linda and Linda, rather self-consciously, returned her smile.

"Is that a new dress?" Anna asked pleasantly.

Linda nodded, then remembered guiltily that it really was not new. Slowly, she stammered, "It's—it's new for me. Mother made it from another dress."

"It looks nice anyway," Anna responded warmly.

Linda was glad she had told the truth, but somehow the dress seemed to lose some of its importance.

When they arrived at Brother Harold and Sister Joyce's home, Linda offered to help set the table.

"Let me get you an apron," Anna offered. "Or did you bring one along?"

"No, Mother said I didn't need to bring one this time," Linda quickly answered. "I'll be careful."

"You may have one of our aprons," Anna persisted.

"No, I'll do without," Linda repeated. But an uneasy feeling came to her as she watched Anna, who was older than herself, tie an apron around her own waist.

The dinner smelled so good that Linda's mouth watered. Anna's little brother must have been hungry too, for as soon as the blessing was asked, he reached eagerly for a piece of bread, knocking over his cup of juice.

"Timmy," his mother gently scolded. "You must wait until I can help you."

Anna whispered to Linda, "Timmy upsets his cup so often."

Linda giggled, then whispered back, "I probably did too when I was a baby."

Um-m, the chicken was delicious! Linda

took another bite, relishing the flavor. She dipped her spoon into her potatoes, coating them with the rich, dark gravy. "I'm glad I didn't wear an apron after all," she thought as she reached for her glass of juice. Slowly she took a sip, then absent-mindedly set it down again.

But, oh, no! It slipped and spilled. Orange juice ran under her plate and onto her dress. There was even juice in the pickle dish.

Linda's face flushed hot red as she got up from her chair. If only she could hide!

"It happens to all of us," Anna's mother said gently in a comforting voice as she wiped up the mess. "Don't let it bother you."

"I'm sorry," Linda murmured in embarrassment as with downcast eyes she returned to her place at the table.

When dinner was over and the girls were cleaning the table, Anna asked Linda kindly, "Did you get something on your sleeve?"

Quickly, Linda inspected the underside of her sleeve and discovered a big spot of gravy. "It looks like I did," she returned in a voice that was quiet and meek.

"Here, I'll help you wash it off," Anna offered. But though the girls rubbed and

*Linda inspected
the underside
of her sleeve.*

rubbed, the stubborn brown spot persisted
in staying.

"We will have to just leave it," Linda
spoke in a dejected voice. "There are juice

stains on the front of my dress, too, so I guess it doesn't really matter."

That evening a different Linda sat in church—a Linda whose mind was on the service and on the Word of God that was being presented. She did not want to look down and see the juice or gravy stains on her dress, and she did not feel grown up or important at all.

That evening when the family was home from church, Mother called Linda into her bedroom. Looking kindly into Linda's unhappy face she asked, "Can you tell me what has been bothering you today?"

"I wish you hadn't made me this dress!" Linda burst out tearfully.

"Why?" Mother questioned gently.

When Linda did not answer, Mother asked, "Are you sure it's the dress that is making you unhappy, or is it that you have been thinking too highly of it?"

Linda looked at Mother miserably, without replying.

"When I saw you admiring your dress the first time," Mother continued, "I was afraid that you were proud of it. Don't you think we should shorten the sleeves a little to remind you that being proud always brings trouble?''

Humbly, Linda nodded her head, yes. As she said good night to Mother and left her room, Linda felt greatly relieved. Once again her heart was light. The uneasy feeling was gone. She was even glad that Mother was going to alter the dress sleeves so it would be just like her other ones.

13

Plans

Spring was a beautiful season! It did not come early in the far north, but when spring arrived, everything seemed to come alive at once. The trees were covered with soft green as new leaves unfurled from bursting buds. The air was scented with the fragrance of early flowers, and the new green grass that pushed it's way through the brown mat of last year's growth displayed lovely, delicate colors.

And oh, the music of the birds! How sweet to hear their warbles and trills as they flitted in the branches of the saskatoon bushes.

The deep blue May sky dazzled with brightness as the sun shone day after day. The mornings that started out cool had, by midmorning, a warmth that gave promise of a summer close at hand.

"I believe today would be a good day to plant our garden," Father announced at the breakfast table. "Before I came in this morning I took the hoe and checked the garden, and I believe it is dry enough to plant. Would it suit you today, Mother?"

"Yes, we'll make it suit," Mother answered pleasantly. "We'll just leave our Saturday's work go this time. It is more important to get the garden planted."

Dishes were hurriedly done while Mother sorted through her seed box, choosing the seeds to be planted.

"Where is a sharp knife?" Rodney asked breathlessly as he burst into the kitchen. "I need one to help cut potatoes for planting."

"There is one in the top drawer," Mother replied. "Please be careful, Son. I don't want you to cut yourself."

"I'll be careful," Rodney promised as he dashed out the door, letting it slam shut behind him.

"I'm ready to go to the garden," Mother announced as she placed the seed packets into a pail. "Bring your sweaters, girls. It may be a little chilly at first."

Raymond was tilling the garden. Martha helped Father unwind the twine and secure the marker for the first row. With quick smooth strikes, Father's hoe cut into the soil, leaving a long, even row stretching ahead of him. Linda, Rodney, and Joanna helped Mother drop seeds into the rows. Even Donnie tried to help.

The garden rang with laughter, happy chatter, and singing as everyone worked together. At dinnertime, the hungry, weary family looked with satisfaction across the garden with its long, evenly-planted rows.

"It looks so nice," Martha commented as she stretched her aching back.

"But God must give the increase," Father stated seriously. "All our morning's work would be in vain if God didn't send the rains and sunshine. It reminds me of a verse in Psalm 67 which says, 'Then shall the earth yield her increase; and God, even our own God, shall bless us.' "

The days continued to get warmer and soon it was comfortable to slip out of the house in the early morning dawn without a jacket.

"O Mother, guess what," Linda panted as she dashed indoors one morning and paused to catch her breath.

"What, Dear? What have you seen this morning?" Mother asked as she smiled at her daughter.

"The garden seeds are growing!" Linda's eyes shone with excitement. "I've been checking them, and this morning for the first time I've noticed the plants peeping through. I could see little bits of green along the whole row."

"Isn't that nice! I'll have to come out with you and see. I think we will have time yet before breakfast."

Mother moved the kettle of hot cereal toward the back of the wood stove, and Linda skipped along beside Mother down the tree-bordered path to the garden. There, straight down a row, they could see a line of tiny green plants. Mother and daughter reveled in the wonder and beauty of it as the moisture on the plants caught the morning sun and sparkled like jewels.

"Now we must hurry," Mother stated, "so breakfast will be ready when Father comes in from the barn."

"I'll set the table, quickly," Linda offered generously. Her shoes slapped the hardened dirt path and echoed behind her as she ran to the house. Breathlessly, she entered the kitchen and quickly swished her hands in the wash basin. "I'll see how much I can get done before Mother gets here," she decided.

That morning the conversation around the breakfast table was of the growing garden. "If we can see the rows now, we should start hoeing beside the plants," Father stated. "The ground seems to have a thin crust, and if we loosen it the rest of the seeds will be better able to come through." Looking at Mother, Father continued, "Maybe Raymond, Martha, and Linda can start doing that this morning. I need to go into town for some parts I have ordered for the field seeder. If we work at the hoeing some each day, it won't take long to go over the whole garden," Father smiled.

Raymond, Martha, and Linda enjoyed working in the garden. The *chop, chop, chop* of their hoes could be heard as they worked steadily, leaving behind a neat row of hoed soil. The frail green plants looked sturdier and greener now, against the darker, freshly-turned earth.

Halfway through the morning Rodney came out to the garden. "Mother says that as soon as you each finish your row you can stop for the morning."

"Good! My arms are getting tired, and the rows are getting longer!" Linda laughed.

A little before dinner, Father came back from town with the seeder parts. "Rodney," he called, "take Mother the mail. There's a letter that she will want to read."

Eagerly Mother opened the letter from her sister, glad for news from their far-away relatives.

"Listen to this!" she told the children. Mother's eyes sparkled as she glanced up from the letter. "Uncle Verns are planning to visit us the third week in June, Lord willing. Isn't that nice! They are planning to stay one week. My, it will be nice to see them again!" she exclaimed as she folded the letter.

"Were you glad for the letter?" Father's

eyes twinkled as he sat down to the dinner table.

"Glad? Why, yes! And I've been thinking of all the things we should do before Uncle Verns come," Mother answered with a smile.

"I've been thinking the same thing," Father commented, "especially since you and I have decided to build a garage. If we put up the outside walls, when Verns come, they can help pour the cement for the floor.

"I have another question," Father continued, as he spooned potatoes onto his plate. Looking at the children, he asked, "How would you like to live in the garage when it is finished?"

"In the garage!" Raymond replied in disbelief. "It would be too small, wouldn't it?"

"I don't think so," Father smiled. "As soon as dinner's over, let's go out to the spot Mother and I have picked out, and I'll show you."

It did not take long for the family to finish their meal. Everyone was eager to go with Father. Together they walked to the building site.

"All right," Father said as he drew a line

in the dirt, "I'll show you what Mother and I are planning." He took a few more steps and drew another line. Measuring distances by counting his steps, Father drew more lines in the dirt. Then he explained. "In this southeast corner would be the boys' bedroom. The girls' bedroom would be next, and in this northeast corner would be Mother's and mine.

"Against the north wall and our bedroom wall would be a small washroom. The rest of the area, facing the road, would be our kitchen and living area. We would put the cupboards against the wall facing the road, and the wood stove would be in the corner by the boys' bedroom."

"Just think, a new house!" Joanna hopped up and down in excitement.

Father smiled at her excitement and kindly said, "It will be a new house plus a warm one, but we will just be making the walls out of rough sawed lumber. Our idea is to live in it for a few years then when we are able to build a new house, we would use this for a garage."

"I don't care," Linda said. "It will still be nice."

"We'll need hard workers to help us," Father told them. "Are you all willing?"

"I'll help," Raymond declared promptly. He liked the idea, too.

"So will I." Martha, who was hesitant at first, was beginning to feel excited.

"Linda and I could help, too," Rodney offered importantly.

"Let's remember," Father told them, "It will take long hard hours of work, but if each one is willing to help, I believe we can finish it before winter. School is out for the summer, so you will be free to help every day."

"We will help!" they all chorused eagerly.

Sheepshearing

Baa. Baa. Baa. The lambs bleated plaintively as they milled around in confusion, trying to find their mothers. Rodney felt sorry for the little lambs as he watched them going in circles. Today was sheepshearing day, and Father and Raymond had just finished separating the lambs from their mothers.

Rodney jumped down from the gate where he had been watching. Closing the door to the sheep barn, he went to find Father. As he rounded the corner of the barn to go to the corrals where the sheep were waiting to be sheared, he almost collided with Raymond, who was carrying a wooden gate.

"Good, you can help me carry this; it isn't the lightest," Raymond grinned at Rodney.

Obligingly, Rodney picked up the tail end, and straining every muscle, he manfully helped. It made him feel good that he could help his big brother, but before they had reached the sheep run his arms were aching. It was with relief that he could finally set his end down. Together the boys slipped the gate between the corral fence and the sheep run fence.

"Thanks so much for helping me," Raymond smiled. "These long gates are so awkward to carry by yourself."

"I'm glad I almost bumped into you," Rodney grinned back. "I was glad to help."

With the sheep run completed, all Raymond needed to do was keep the run filled with unsheared sheep. When Father was ready for a sheep, Raymond would open the gate beside the shearing platform and release one sheep at a time for shearing.

Now began the excitement of the day. Eagerly the children waited for Father to begin.

"All right, I'm ready," Father called. Raymond opened the gate to let the first sheep out. Father was waiting. With a quick grab and flip, the bewildered sheep landed on the shearing platform. Raymond quickly closed the gate and hurried over to help Father. The sheep gave a few bewildered bleats, and then lay still.

With quick smooth strokes Father's shears bit into the wool, not too deep to cut into the sheep's skin, only deep enough to cut away the thick layer of wool. Raymond never tired of watching Father as ripple after ripple of wool lay back, revealing the rough sheep skin. He felt it was something he could never do himself, and he wondered how Father could know so exactly how deep to cut. Once in a while, however, a small red spot appeared when Father clipped too close.

Soon the first sheep was finished and Father let the shorn sheep down from the shearing platform. Off it ran into the pasture. Rodney laughed aloud as he watched the shorn sheep kicking up its heels. It looked so funny!

"Rodney, you may start filling the wool bag," Father called as he grabbed the second

*Rodney
scrambled
up the ladder
with the fleece.*

sheep. "If you bag each fleece as soon as it is cut, you won't get behind."

Rodney climbed down from his perch on the fence and picked up the fleece. Father had built an eight-foot-high platform with four tall, sturdy poles as legs. A ladder ran up one side and a round hole had been cut from the center of the platform. From this hole hung a huge, seven-foot long burlap bag. Rodney scrambled up the ladder with the fleece and watched as it fell with a gentle plop into the empty bag. Almost as soon as he had climbed back down, Father had another fleece waiting for him.

At first it was fun, but as the morning wore on his steps became slower, and he could no longer keep up. Dropping another fleece into the rapidly filling bag, Rodney glanced longingly toward the house. "If only Linda or Joanna would come," he thought.

At that moment, the door of the house opened and the girls came out carrying something. Mother and Donnie followed.

"Good," he brightened, "I hope they have something for me." With renewed energy he climbed down the ladder.

When Father saw Mother and the girls,

he called to Raymond. "Don't let any more sheep in. It's time for a rest."

"We thought you might be hungry," Mother called cheerily.

"We are," Father answered as he climbed the fence, picked up Donnie, and tossed him into the air. Donnie squealed with delight.

The boys left the sheep pens and soon everyone was seated on the grass. As Rodney waited for the wet washcloth with which to wash his hands, he eyed the rolls hungrily. They smelled so good!

"You look tired and hungry," Mother smiled as she handed Rodney a warm cinnamon-filled roll. "I see you've been busy," she went on as she glanced up at the wool bag.

"Yes, he has helped real well," Father said. "But when we get back to work I think one of the girls should stay and help. Can you spare one?"

"I believe so. Linda may stay if she's needed," Mother replied.

Father reached for another roll and refilled his glass with milk. "We'd better get back to our job," he announced as he finished his snack.

Fleece Lessons

Up and down, up and down Rodney and Linda jumped. The afternoon sun shone warmly, making it hot inside the wool bag. Up and down, up and down, compacting the wool to make room for more fleeces.

"Let's rest," Linda panted as she flopped her arms over the side of the platform to catch the gentle breezes. The wool felt rough and greasy from dirt and bits of burrs that were caught in it, but Linda did not mind. She loved the wooly smell and even if it was hot work, she enjoyed helping. With both Rodney and her working together they could easily keep up with Father and have time to pack the wool.

"Don't bag any more fleeces," Father called above the snip, snip of the shears as he took quick, smooth strokes. "I want to save the rest for our own needs."

Finally the last sheep was on the shearing platform. With weary but happy feelings, everyone watched the last shorn sheep run bleating toward the others in the pasture.

Father climbed up the platform to the fleece bag. "Raymond," he called, "I need your help to close this bag."

Quickly Raymond hurried up the ladder to Father, and grabbing the end of the rope drawstring, he braced his feet and helped Father pull. Slowly the opening closed. While Raymond hung on to keep the rope from slipping back, Father skillfully secured the knots.

"There, that's finished," Father declared with satisfaction, as he lowered the wool bag onto the waiting wagon below. "Tomorrow we will ship our wool out on the morning train."

The sun had dropped low in the west. As it slipped behind the trees, the sky blazed with color. "Another beautiful sunset!" Father spoke in worshipful tones. "God has given us another lovely ending to a beautiful day."

Together they watched the colors fade into a deep pink. As the twilight gathered, Father and Raymond packed the wool they had kept for their own use into gunny sacks. Stars twinkled in the clear sky above as Father and Raymond walked to the house.

"Girls, girls, good morning. It's time to get up. We have a busy day ahead," Linda heard Mother's gentle voice the next morning.

"I'm so tired and stiff," Linda mumbled sleepily to herself as she slowly dragged herself out of bed. When she remembered that this was the day they were going to clean sheep wool, she was suddenly wide awake.

"I let you sleep later than usual," Mother smiled at Linda as she entered the kitchen. "Father had to eat early to get the wool to the station on time. Your breakfast is on the back of the stove. Joanna and Rodney haven't eaten yet, either. As soon as you three have eaten," Mother continued, "I want you to wash dishes and make your beds. Martha and I will be working out by the pump."

Mother left the house, and Linda started dishing out three bowls of hot, steaming cereal. She set the bowls on the table and went to get the pitcher of milk that Mother had left cooling in a bucket of water. When she returned, Rodney and Joanna were waiting at the table. In record time they finished eating and hurriedly did their morning's work.

"I wonder if they've washed much wool yet," Rodney commented as he hung up his dish towel.

"We're almost ready to go out," Linda answered. Quickly she put the last dishes into the cupboard. Glancing in satisfaction at the neat kitchen, Linda closed the door and hurried out to the pump, followed by Rodney.

"We need you," Martha called when she saw them coming. She was busily checking each fleece for burrs or tiny twigs which had become caught in the wool. These needed to be removed before they could be washed.

Rodney watched as Mother took a piece of homemade soap and lathered the wool.

Then back and forth, back and forth, she rubbed the wool on the scrub board. When it was clean she dipped it up and down in a tub of clear water. After she had rinsed it the second time, she took the snowy white fleece and hung it over the corral fence to dry.

"This is a lot of work," Linda declared.

"Yes, it is," Mother remarked. "And this is only the beginning. After the wool is all washed and dried we will store it until this fall when our summer's work is over. Then we will work with it some more."

"I like to watch Father card the wool," Martha interrupted. "He can do it fast and never gets the carders caught."

Mother smiled when she remembered Martha's frustrated attempts at carding. Things would begin to go smoothly for her, and then the carder wires would get caught together.

"I forget what carders are," Joanna looked perplexed. "What are they, Mother?"

"Rodney, run to Father's shop and bring a pair. They're hanging by the cupboard," Mother said.

Soon he was back with two square wooden paddles with handles. "I can't get them apart," Rodney said as he handed them to Mother.

Mother took the carders, pushed them in opposite directions, and lifted them apart. Joanna crowded close to see. On each carder were short, stiff, bent wires. They came straight up about a third of an inch, then bent over to form a shape like an upside-down capital L.

"You take a piece of wool like this," Mother told her interested listeners as she put a small piece of wool on one of the carders, "then you pull the carders in opposite directions."

Mother demonstrated as she placed the second carder on top of the first and pulled a couple of strokes, catching the soft wool in the hooks. She handed the wool to Joanna.

"Oh, it's so soft." Joanna's eyes twinkled excitedly as she rubbed it on her cheek. "May I keep it?"

"Yes, you may," Mother smiled. Handing the carders back to Rodney, she picked up another fleece and began washing it. "Put the carders back, Son," she instructed, "so we will be able to find them when they're needed."

"Did you know the Bible talks about women and their work with wool?" Mother asked the girls.

"It does?" Martha looked surprised. "I didn't know that."

"It is found in the last chapter of Proverbs. Maybe this evening you can find it and read it. That chapter describes a virtuous woman or a righteous woman. One verse says, 'She seeketh wool, and flax, and worketh willingly with her hands.' Another verse says, 'She layeth her hands to the spindle, and her hands hold the distaff.'"

"That's talking about the spinning wheel," Martha spoke, surprised. "Aren't the spindle and distaff part of the spinning wheel?"

"You're right," Mother smiled. "The spindle twists the wool thread while the distaff holds the wool."

Mother stopped to hang another fleece on the corral fence. "These verses are telling us how the virtuous woman provides for her family. She isn't idle but does her work willingly. It's important that you girls learn this," Mother encouraged.

"It helps me to be more diligent when I

know that God wants me to be," Martha said quietly. "I'll admit I could do better."

"I could, too." Linda thought guiltily of all the times she had grumbled or had not done her work right. It gave her a happy feeling to remember that they had cleaned the kitchen up right that morning.

Mother smiled warmly at her daughters, and they returned her smile.

Working Together

Time was swiftly passing, and the days sped by as the family worked steadily on the new house. There was only one more week until Uncle Verns would be coming. The new house was framed, but would the walls be finished before Uncle Verns arrived?

Eeec-ch! Eeec-ch! The screeching of the saw blade was deafening as it cut through the wood. Rodney and Joanna watched in fascination from a safe distance as Father moved the lever that guided the log through the blade.

Eee-ch! Eeec-ch! the saw screamed as one

long bark slab fell from the log. Father pushed the lever the opposite way, and the log carriage started backward. *Twang!* went the saw blade as the log brushed past it.

Father turned the log one-fourth turn with another lever, and again the saw's screams filled the air as the log went forward and backward, making another side smooth. Twice more Father turned the log and ran it through the saw blade, leaving it square instead of round. Father then ran the square log through the blade, slicing it into inch thick boards.

Raymond picked up each newly-made board and placed it neatly on the waiting wagon.

As soon as one log was finished, Father sawed another one. Slowly the pile of unsawed logs grew smaller while the slab piles grew higher.

"I think Father's waving for us to come," Rodney told Joanna from where they were watching. "You'd better stay here, though, until I come back. You might get hurt."

Joanna nodded her head in agreement, not at all eager to go closer to the noisy sawmill.

Rodney hurried toward Father, picking his way across broken slabs and piles of sawdust. When he was almost there, Father turned and shouted something to him.

"What?" Rodney shouted back, unable to hear.

Eee-ch! Eee-ch! the sawmill screamed as a long dark slab fell from the log.

Father shook his head and motioned for him not to come any nearer.

Rodney stopped and waited, watching as the log buzzed through the saw, sending tiny wood shavings flying in every direction. Then Father walked over to Rodney.

"Would you bring Raymond and me a drink, Son? Tell Mother I sent you."

"Okay," Rodney answered.

"I must get Father a drink," Rodney panted as he reached Joanna. "Will you go with me?"

It seemed a long way back to the sawmill, as together Joanna and Rodney lugged the jug of fresh, cold water Mother had given them.

"Let's rest," Joanna pleaded. "It's so-o heavy."

Rodney reluctantly agreed. He was eager to get back to the activity at the sawmill.

Raymond hurried to meet them. "Just what I've been waiting for!" He reached for the jug and took a long drink. "Does that ever taste good! Thanks a lot." He smiled at Rodney and Joanna.

Joanna beamed happily.

"You're welcome," Rodney returned,

glad that he had been able to help.

"I'll take the jug to Father," Raymond told them. "You be sure you stay away from the saw."

The children nodded and hurried to their watching spot.

By midafternoon the last of the logs was sawed, and the boards were neatly stacked on the wagon. How quiet and still the outdoors seemed, for the saw that had been screaming and screeching now stood silent though it still seemed to be ringing in their ears.

Father and Raymond drove the loaded wagon up to the building site, and before long a different noise shattered the stillness. *Pound. Pound. Pound.* The hammers echoed and re-echoed steadily as the newly sawed boards were nailed to the house frame.

"You can help me hold these boards," Raymond called to Rodney who was racing back and forth inside the house. "I need someone with a lot of energy."

Rodney hurried over. With a grin, he picked up one end of a board and held it dutifully against the studs for Raymond to measure. Peeping over the top, he could see

Mother and Martha busily hammering away on another wall. Even Linda was scurrying back and forth, carrying nails and helping to bring and hold boards. Father was sawing boards to the correct size beside the wagon.

"Here's another board we'll need to measure," Raymond said, interrupting Rodney's thoughts. Expertly, Raymond marked the board and took it over to Father to saw.

"This place looks like an anthill," Martha remarked to Mother while they waited for Father to measure and saw more boards for them. "Everyone's busy working or running here and there," Martha laughed.

"Yes, I guess it does," Mother smiled in answer. "The ant sets a good example for us to follow."

"How?" Linda stopped sorting nails to ask.

"A verse in Proverbs says, 'Go to the ant, thou sluggard; consider her ways, and be wise,' " Mother explained. "All summer the ants work, bringing in food, preparing their homes for winter, and taking care of their young. We are to take a lesson from their industry and do the same, working and providing for ourselves."

Daylight was beginning to fade as the sun dropped lower and lower in the sky. Martha and Linda left the house and went to set the table for supper. Rodney gathered up the tools, while Mother and Raymond nailed the last measured boards in place.

From the corner where Joanna and Donnie were stacking their wooden blocks, Joanna was singing. Donnie was singing along with his own special words and notes, "When we all work together, together, together; / When we all work together, how happy we'll be. / When we all work together, together, ... ," Over and over she sang the words, busy with her blocks.

"Are you coming along with us?" Father stopped beside Joanna and brushed the sawdust off of Donnie before picking him up. "It's time to eat supper."

Joanna slipped her hand in Father's big one and skipped along, still singing, "When we all work together, together, together; / When we all work together, how happy we'll be."

Father smiled down at her bobbing head and turned to Mother. "How true; happiness comes from working together. We certainly have gotten a lot of work done today. The Lord willing, we will be able to finish sheathing the house by next week."

Raymond straightened his tired, drooping shoulders when he heard Father's praise. He did not seem quite as tired as he had before; a warm feeling of contentment crept over him.

Company

At last the big day for Uncle Verns' arrival dawned. The hours dragged slowly by as the children, with keen anticipation, awaited the arrival of their cousins. "When will they come? Will it be soon?" the younger children kept asking Mother.

"Let's go check the strawberries. There should be some ripening," Mother suggested to Rodney and Joanna in the late afternoon.

"Here's one," Joanna announced excitedly. "Look how nice and red it is!"

"And here's some more," Rodney told Mother, holding back the leaves for Mother to see.

Mother and the children were so intent on finding strawberries that they missed seeing the approaching car until a horn honked. Glancing up, they saw a car turn into their lane.

"Uncle Verns!" Rodney shouted.

"Yes, I believe it is." Mother stood up quickly and brushed the straw from her dress, and then she hurried toward the house. Slowly Rodney and Joanna followed, suddenly becoming shy at the thought of meeting the cousins they hardly knew.

"It is so good to see you," Mother greeted Aunt Sue warmly. "How the boys have grown! Can this really be George?" She looked up at the tall youth.

Arnold and Greg were next in line, and Mother shook hands with them. "Where's Thomas—oh, he's with Rodney," Mother smiled after the two boys who were already heading for the barn.

Self-consciously, Betty and Joanna, the two little girls, clung to their mothers, soberly eyeing one another.

Father, Uncle Vern, and the boys, soon went to inspect the new building, while

Mother, Aunt Sue and the girls entered the house to finish preparing supper.

"I'm glad you plan to stay for a week," Mother told Aunt Sue. "The time will pass too quickly to suit us. Our visitors are usually few and far between here in this far north country."

The next morning at the breakfast table, Uncle Vern turned to Father. "We don't want to interfere with any work you have to do. Rather, if we can help you in any way, we want to do that."

"I was planning on your help," Father admitted, laughing. "Four strong boys should be able to get a lot of work done."

"What do you have in mind?" Uncle Vern urged.

"Well, we must haul rocks for the house floor before we can pour the cement. Does that sound all right to you?" Father asked.

"Certainly. That will be something new and I'm sure our boys will enjoy it," Uncle Vern answered.

"May I go, too?" Linda pleaded after the men had left the house. "Please!"

"If Martha goes along, you may," Mother consented.

"Martha. Martha." Linda hurried off, calling her sister. "Where are you?"

"In the boys' bedroom," came Martha's answer.

"O Martha, don't you want to go along and help load rocks? Mother said we may."

"Well, I suppose," Martha answered slowly. "Help me finish making these beds first, though, and then I'll be ready."

Laughing and talking, the cousins bounced along as they rode on the bumpy, jostling wagon. Soon they had covered the three miles to their minister's farm where they were going to load rocks. The hilly farmland was dotted with rock piles, and Brother Wayne was only too happy to get rid of some of them.

Bang. Bang. Bang. Rocks thudded noisily into the empty wagon. *Bang. Bang. Bang.* The challenge was keen to fill the wagon quickly. Soon the willing, eager workers had the wagon loaded. Mounting the mounded rocks, each chose his own "chair" for the ride home.

Enthusiasm waned with the unloading, nor was the excitement as high to collect the second load.

Company

"May I stay home?" Linda begged after the wagon was emptied the second time.

"No," Mother answered. "You wanted to help, and you must stay with the job until it is finished." Mother smiled kindly into Linda's tired face. "This jug of water and these cookies may help to renew everyone's energy."

Linda trudged outside, carrying the cookies and water to the waiting wagon. There was little talking or laughing as the weary group went for the last load. Silently they munched their cookies and rested their weary arms and backs.

At last the wagon was loaded, and they were homeward bound.

"We won't unload this today," Father announced to his exhausted helpers. "I really appreciate what you have done. Now the floor is almost ready for cementing."

The next morning after family worship, Father announced, "I have some news I think everyone would be interested in hearing." His eyes twinkled mysteriously.

"What? Tell us," the children chorused.

"Since everyone worked so hard yesterday, we will take the day off and go to the

159

lake."

"Goody! Goody! Oh, goody!" The younger children jumped around in excitement.

George looked at Raymond, his eyes sparkling. "Now that's what I call good pay!"

Raymond laughed. He, too, was glad to have the day off. The last weeks had been extremely busy, building the garage and preparing for Uncle Verns' arrival.

Mother, Aunt Sue, and the girls scurried around, packing the picnic dinner and washing the breakfast dishes.

"Where's your car?" George looked around, perplexed, when they were getting ready to leave.

"We don't have any," Raymond answered slowly. "We usually use that." He pointed to the tractor parked by the new building. Half-embarrassed, he kicked at a stone with the toe of his shoe. Usually he did not mind using the tractor, but somehow, today, he hated to tell his cousin they had no vehicle.

"That would be fun," George quickly responded.

"Everyone ready?" Father called as he carried the box of food to Uncle Vern's car.

"Yes," Mother answered. "Come, girls, let's get into the car now.

Turning to the older boys, Father asked teasingly, "Do you want to climb into the trunk with the food?" Then he added seriously, "Would you mind riding there? If you don't, we can't all go in the car."

"It sounds like fun to me," George declared as he headed for the car trunk. Raymond, Greg, and Arnold followed and squeezed in beside George.

"I wish Thomas and I could ride in the trunk, too," Rodney expressed in disappointment, as he climbed into the front seat of the car.

"I do, too," Thomas echoed.

After the boys were given firm instruction to sit still, the loaded car left for the lake.

Dust from the gravel road rolled out in clouds from the rear wheels of the car. The boys sat tightly wedged together, holding up their hands in an effort to keep the trunk lid from hitting them too hard on their heads. They started to laugh hilariously.

The
boys
laughed
hilariously.

"This is the most fun we've ever had," Arnold said when he could control his laughter enough to talk.

Raymond grinned back. He, too, was enjoying the ride, and his cousins' frank pleasure in the situation made the miserable feeling he had earlier, vanish.

The car slowed down and descended the hill that led to the blue lake below. The instant the car stopped, the boys scrambled out, eager to explore.

What fun they had that day! Wading in the lake's shallow edge, running races and playing games. Even fishing without catching any fish had been fun. In the late afternoon, the happy, contented parents and children reloaded the car, each finding a little place for himself.

"Good-by, good-by," Greg and Arnold waved from the trunk of the car as it climbed the hill to the main road. Below them lay the peaceful pine-bordered lake which would not soon be forgotten.

Slab Shack

How quickly the week flew by. All too
soon Uncle Verns were saying, "Good-by,"
and leaving for their southern home. The
smooth, freshly cemented, new house floor
showed that they had not been idle during
their stay.

"Thank you for your much-appreciated
help," Father said to Uncle Vern.

"I'm glad we were able to help you. It
made our trip north even more worthwhile."

The family waved fond good-bys as the
car drove out the lane and turned onto the
road. Faintly the children could see their

cousins still waving back to them as the car climbed the hill. Then, disappearing over the crest, the car was gone.

"It's so boring around here!" Linda complained that afternoon as she flopped down on a kitchen chair. "There just isn't anything to do!"

"Shall I find something for you to do?" Mother asked. "It wouldn't be too hard for me."

"No, I mean it's no fun with Uncle Verns gone. I wish they could have stayed another week," Linda returned sulkily.

Mother looked sternly at Linda, then said, "Why don't you take Father and Raymond a lunch? They're working at the sawmill."

Mother's look silenced Linda, and she guiltily nodded her consent to take the lunch.

Walking through the wild grasses and flowers washed away Linda's unhappy, restless feelings. Overhead the sun shone warmly while a gentle breeze played softly, making the flowers nod and sway to each other. Butterflies fluttered from one flower to the next. A bumble bee buzzed near her and Linda moved out of its way and watched it land on a blossom nearby. As she approached the sawmill, Linda could hear Father and Raymond working. The harsh, rasping sound of Father filing on the saw blade sent shivers up and down her spine.

"I have something for you to eat," Linda called cheerfully.

"What did you bring?" Raymond wondered. "I'm famished."

After they thanked God for the food, Father joined Raymond as he reached for a sandwich.

"Say," Raymond turned to Father, "what are we going to do with all these wood slabs?"

"Probably use some for firewood. Why?"

"Well, I just thought of an idea. Could David and I build a little shack somewhere? We could use the nails you don't want for the garage," Raymond spoke eagerly.

Father sat thoughtfully considering Raymond's idea. He reached for another sandwich, then handed his glass to Linda for her to refill with water. "I don't see why that wouldn't be possible," he said at last. "I believe we could work it out so that every week you could have some free time to work on it."

"Thank you, Father!" Raymond smiled his enthusiastic appreciation. Plans were already forming in his mind that he could hardly wait to share with his friend, and neighbor David.

The next morning Raymond stood at the window watching the rain run in tiny streams down the glass. "I'm so glad it's raining!" he exclaimed.

"Why?" Martha asked as she paused beside the table.

"Maybe I will have time to see if David will want to build the slab house with me," Raymond answered.

Later at the breakfast table, Raymond asked Father, "Are we going to work on the new house today?"

"I would like to. We should start boarding up the inside walls so we can put in the insulation."

Raymond tried not to show his disappointment. How he wanted to get started on the shack! Then he remembered his promise to help on the new building, and pushing aside his own wishes and plans, he answered, "I guess we should start to do that—but what are we going to use for insulation?"

"Wait and see," Father said mysteriously. "I'll give you a puzzle to think about. Maybe you can come up with the answer. Here is the puzzle: we have so much of it lying around on our farm, we don't know what to do with it."

Father's words kept repeating themselves in Raymond's mind. "So much of it! So much of it! What could it be?" he wondered.

Outside the rain drummed on the roof. It was nice to be able to work inside and hear the music of rain overhead.

"Do you know what Father was talking about?" Martha asked Raymond as they hammered nails.

"No, do you?"

Martha shook her head. "Listen to this," she said with a smile.

> "It's lying all around,
> Right at our very door;
> It's over-running the farm,
> But I can't guess any more!"

Raymond laughed. "You and your rhymes! But listen to this one.

"Can you guess
What it could be?
Don't you know?
Can you not see?"

That's pretty good," Martha laughed. "Seriously though, I wonder what Father means. I hope I can figure it out before we insulate."

All morning they hammered away. Father kept ahead of them, putting up the tarpaper over which they nailed the boards.

"Look, Raymond," Martha called. "There is tarpaper under the outside boards, too, and now we are doing the same thing inside. How will we get insulation between these two walls with both sides boarded up?"

"That I don't know," Raymond admitted, perplexed. "Guess we'll have to wait and see."

Father overheard them talking. His eyes twinkled merrily, and he gave them a smile.

After dinner, Father asked Raymond, "How would you like to scout out a place for your shack this afternoon?"

"Oh, could I?"

"It's just raining lightly and it shouldn't be too wet under the trees. There are some other things I should take care of, so you may have the afternoon off," Father replied.

"May I go and tell David about our plans when I've found a place?" Raymond requested eagerly.

"Yes," Father consented. "But be back in time for chores."

Raymond's feet fairly flew as he ran past the barn, the saw mill, and down the trail which ran along the forest's edge. Coming to the end of the field, Raymond followed the trail as it turned into the forest.

"I need four big pines fairly close together," he decided, "on which to nail our slabs." A sweet mossy smell rose to meet him as he entered the pines. Carefully he looked around trying to select the best spot.

"This is it!" he whistled aloud in excitement. Before him towered four tall pines. "Just the right size!" he exclaimed as he measured the distance between them. "I can't wait to tell David." Before going on to David's home, Raymond observed the spot well so he would be able to find it again. The sun was peeking through the clouds now. It looked as though the rain was over.

Raymond walked across a narrow field,

crossed a fence, and started up the road. The two-mile walk to David's house gave him plenty of time to think, and he was so occupied with planning, he was surprised at how quickly he found himself climbing up the gently sloping hill to his friend's house. Blackie raced out to meet him, barking and snapping at his heels.

"Raymond!" David called, surprised. "What are you doing?"

"Trying to find you," Raymond grinned.

Excitedly Raymond told David of his project and invited him to help.

"That sounds like fun," David answered. "I'm sure Mother won't care, but I'll ask her anyway," and he ran to the house.

"Mother says it's all right with her, so let's go," David reported when he came back.

"We will have to bring the slabs by wagon," Raymond declared as the friends schemed together. "I'm sure Father will let me."

"It wouldn't take us too long to build, once we have the slabs there. When can we start?" David asked.

"Father said he will give me some time every week, so probably we can start next week," Raymond responded. "It will likely take us a while, especially if we want a window and a door."

"And if we cover our roof with moss so it won't leak," David added.

The boys arrived at the spot Raymond had chosen, and enthusiastically discussed possibilities. Finally David said, "If you have to be home in time to do your chores, I should be going." He looked at his watch. "It's already four-thirty. Just let me know when you plan to start."

David took a few steps, then stopped. "Thanks for asking me to help. We don't live on a farm and with my father working away from home all the time, my days are pretty long and empty."

"I need you," Raymond smiled. "Besides it will be fun to work together. I'll let you know when we're ready to start building."

"See you then," David called as they parted.

As Raymond walked slowly homeward along the trail, he was thinking of David's words. Although there were times when he would have been glad for a break from the steady work of the farm, yet hard work was rewarding and was far better than idleness. And another blessing he had was that both his parents were Christians, while only David's mother was.

"I have it good!" Raymond spoke aloud. He felt like shouting, "I have the best parents in the world!" Instead he breathed a prayer thanking God for his Christian home and parents. He prayed for David's father, too, that he would become a Christian.

With a light heart, he broke into a run and raced for the barn. He knew that one way he could show his parents how much he appreciated them was by obeying and helping them. He intended not to disappoint them.

H ave you shed some light this day?
A s you worked or as you played?
P utting others first will show,
P lent'ous love for them, you know.
I n the light of God's command,
N oting what He does demand.
E ach day we will help each other,
S acrificing for another.
S haring joyf'lly with our brother.

Happiness

"Sh-h-h! Listen. Hear that bird?" Martha whispered. "I've been sitting here for a while trying to figure out where the bird is. What took you so long in coming?"

"I had to finish folding the towels. Then Mother said we could be free for an hour." Linda spoke softly as she sat down beside Martha.

High up somewhere in the tall pines, they could hear a little bird sing. Its song was short, yet beautiful. The last notes echoed in the stillness. Then again came warbling notes from the hidden singer, loud and clear. The beautiful song made the girls tingle in delight.

With a sigh of contentment, Linda glanced at the forest around her. The pines swayed softly in the breeze, moaning and sighing, while the sunlight filtered through to where they listened, trying to see the exuberant songster.

Again came the clear thrilling song. "O Martha, look quickly!" Linda pointed excitedly. "I see it! I see it! Over on that far branch."

"Sure enough!" Martha saw the bird. "No wonder I couldn't find it. It looks like part of the branch!" she exclaimed.

Once more the liquid notes spilled from the tiny throat; then the singer flew up and away between the pines and out of sight.

"Oh, that was delightful! I love it out here under the pines—there's always something new to see or hear," Linda sighed contentedly. "We will have to ask Father what kind of bird that was. I'd like to know."

"Linda, look at this moss." Martha pointed beside her. "It looks like tiny ferns. I don't remember seeing any like it before. "I know," she spoke enthusiastically, "let's make another moss garden. The one we have in the bowl at home isn't very nice anymore."

The forest floor was covered with a thick layer of moss, and out of the moss grew many varieties of tiny green plants. Martha dug with her fingers into the soft, spongy ground, then carefully she pried loose a big chunk of moss.

"I can hardly wait to show this to Mother! I wonder if she has ever seen such beautiful moss. It will make a lovely garden."

"But we'd better remember to keep it watered," Linda laughed as she hopped from one big clump of moss to the next. "Or it will soon look like our other brown, dried-up garden."

"We should start for home now, Linda. I'm sure our hour will soon be up. I want to plant this in the bowl as soon as we get home." Martha started toward the old logging trail that led to the field.

But Linda kept jumping. It was so much fun to see if she could reach the next clump of moss—then see how far it would sink with her weight on it.

Jump. Jump. Linda sat down to rest a little. Everything was quiet. She looked quickly around but could see nothing of her sister. "I must hurry," Linda thought and started running.

Soon she reached the open field and gave

But Linda kept jumping.

a sigh of relief when she saw Martha far ahead.

"Martha, wait. I'm coming," Linda called loudly. "I must have jumped longer than I thought," Linda panted when she caught up with Martha. She tried to get her breath. "Then I couldn't see you and I had to run."

"Well, next time come when I say; then you won't have to run so hard," Martha scolded teasingly.

The girls walked down the field lane silently, watching their feet scatter the dust in little puffs. Bees were buzzing among the wildflowers which grew everywhere. The scent of wild roses hung in the air. Stopping beside the roses, both girls breathed deeply of their fragrant perfume.

Linda picked up the corners of her apron, fashioned a basket, and carefully started picking some of the prettiest blooms. "I know Mother will like these," she said. "She's not able to come back here very often."

Martha started humming as they continued walking home. When the girls reached the gate, Linda joined Martha and together they sang,

"Heavenly sunlight, heavenly sunlight,
Flooding my soul with glory divine;
Hallelujah! I am rejoicing,
Singing His praises—Jesus is mine!"

Mother opened the screen door as the girls came around the corner of the house. "How sweet to hear you singing," she smiled. "Did you enjoy your afternoon?"

"Oh, yes! And see what we brought back!" Martha exclaimed. "Won't this make a pretty moss garden? I think I'll plant it right now."

Linda opened her apron. "These are for you, Mother. They were so pretty I wanted you to see them."

"Thank you, Dear. That was thoughtful of you," Mother said as she bent to smell the luscious fragrance. "Let's arrange some in a vase, and maybe Martha would want to use some in her moss garden."

Martha was busy at the table when they came in. She had spread a newspaper and was emptying the old moss from the bowl onto the paper. After she had washed the bowl, she carefully took the fresh moss and arranged it in the container, breaking off the edges of the moss to make it fit.

"Let's use a small low vase to hold the roses," Mother suggested as she went to the cupboard to get a suitable one. "Make a little hollowed out place for it in the moss," she instructed, "and Linda, please bring a little water."

Mother poured water into the vase, then Linda arranged the roses. Martha placed the small mirror they had used for a lake partly under one of the roses. Acorns were added for pine cones and the moss was watered.

"That is pretty!" Mother commended the girls warmly. "If you keep it watered, it will be nice for a long time."

"I'm so glad we went!" Linda bubbled over. "It makes me feel all happy inside."

"When we take time to enjoy all the beautiful things that God has created, it makes us think of Him. And when we think of God and what He has done for us, we want to praise Him. That's one reason you feel happy inside," Mother explained. "I think I know another reason. Do you remember what you girls were doing when you came to the house? You were singing. When we sing of our heavenly Father, that brings happiness because when we sing sincerely, we are fellowshiping with God."

That evening the girls remembered the bird that had sung so sweetly for them. "O Father, I wish you could have heard it. Its voice was so clear and beautiful it made me tingle." Linda almost tingled again in remembrance.

"We couldn't find it at first," Martha added. "But then we did see it, and it was rather large and brown like the branch."

Father thought for a moment, then decided that it had probably been a brown thrasher. "The thrasher is one of the prettiest singers you'll hear in the woods. Some people call them the mockingbirds of the north, because they seem to copy other birds' songs as the southern mockingbirds do. They have one of the sweetest bird voices we have in this area." Father smiled at Linda. "I never tire of listening to them."

"We've had such a happy day today," the girls told Father.

"I'm glad to hear that. Every day is happy when we are thankful for whatever the day brings," Father smiled. "Can you think of other things that make a day happy?"

"Kindness, cheerfulness, and obedience bring happiness," Martha stated.

"And singing," Linda added brightly.

"Let's remember these things," Father smiled, "and make every day a happy day."

20

Summer Twilight

It was the middle of summer. Gradually the days had lengthened until it stayed light all day and almost all night. For several hours in the night a faint twilight fell, but it was so light outdoors it seemed as a cloudy day.

"O Mother," Rodney asked breathlessly, "Father is going to stay up late and work. Can we?"

Mother glanced at the clock which indicated that it was already past bedtime. She looked at Rodney and at the light night sky.

"It's like the middle of the day!" Rodney exclaimed persuasively, "And I'm not tired at all."

"I guess it won't matter this time," Mother smiled, "as long as Father says it's all right with him."

"Oh, good!" Rodney dashed outside into the bright night time and raced for the new house.

The lantern hanging in the building made it as light inside as it was outside. High up on a ladder, Father and Raymond were busily nailing boards. After getting Father's consent to stay up awhile longer, Rodney hurried to find Linda and Joanna. He found them down by the garden, making a farm in the tall weeds.

"We may all stay up until Father's finished working," Rodney told them.

"Even Donnie?" Joanna exclaimed.

"No," Rodney answered. "He is already in bed sleeping."

"I think it's so much fun having it light all night that I wish it would be like this all summer," Linda said as she trampled down weeds.

"We want to make a lane and a barn yet,

too," Joanna informed Rodney.

Happy voices and laughter drifted through the still night air to the workers in the new house. "It is beautiful outside tonight," Martha remarked to Mother. Wistfully she looked at the fields and forests that surrounded their farm. Everything was bathed in the strange light of the far north night time—a light that seemed to have a silvery touch to it whose stillness beckoned to her. Longingly she wished she could race across the fields down to the creek and follow it on and on.

"I'm not sleepy, just tired," Martha thought as she carried some boards for nailing.

"God has been good to us," Mother interrupted her thoughts. "The past week has been cloudless, and Father has been able to finish sawing the lumber. The inside walls are almost boarded, and all that is left is insulation, partitions, doors, and windows."

Martha nodded her head in agreement, but her thoughts took a sudden detour. "Insulation! What could Father possibly be using?" Hopelessly she shook her head. She had puzzled over this riddle often in the last number of weeks. She just could not figure it out. How she wished she could!

At eleven-thirty that night, Father nailed the last board into place. Outside, the night was just as bright and clear as it had been earlier, but now everyone was tired enough that even though it was not dark, they were ready to go to bed.

A few hours later a faint twilight stole over the sky and the sleeping farm. For two hours it lasted before the sun arose bright and clear once more.

Late that morning the children awakened. Father had finished the chores and had told Mother that Raymond was free for the rest of the morning and could use the wagon to haul slabs for his house.

"We'll be insulating the new house this afternoon," Mother added after giving Raymond Father's message. "You girls may help Raymond if you want to. This afternoon we will need everyone's help with the insulating."

"Let's help him!" Martha exclaimed. "Do you want us to, Raymond?" Martha asked.

"Sure. Rodney's going to help, and if you and Linda help, too, maybe we could get all the slabs hauled this morning that we need. Let's go, Rodney." Raymond was eager to get started. "Rodney and I will meet you down at the sawmill."

The tractor and wagon were parked by the slab pile, waiting to be filled. The boys began sorting slabs, and when the girls arrived there were a number ready for loading. Up and down, back and forth from the slab pile to the wagon the girls trudged.

"My arms are so tired I don't know if I can lift another slab!" Linda sighed wearily, looking at the pile Raymond had sorted out.

"Let's rest," Martha declared. "I'm tired, too. Come, Rodney, it's break time."

The warm sunshine made the sawdust feel hot where the girls were sitting. Linda wiggled her hands down into the pile to where it was nice and cool. Slowly she raised her fingers, letting it sift through.

"Look at all this sawdust!" she exclaimed. "I wonder what Father will ever do with all of it."

"Sawdust!" Martha almost shouted in excitement. "Sawdust! Raymond, come here. Do you know what Father is going to do with all this sawdust? Just look at these huge piles!''

Linda watched her, puzzled. Why was Martha so excited? Raymond was equally puzzled.

"He'll just leave it here," Linda declared. "That's what you do with sawdust at a sawmill."

But Martha was still excited. "Look at the sawdust, Raymond! Can't you guess what's lying around on our farm that we have so much of we don't know what to do with it?"

Martha was laughing, and the light finally dawned on Raymond. "Oh, no!" he groaned. "Insulation! Why didn't I think of it. Aren't you brilliant!" he teased, laughing with her. "That's why Father put tarpaper on both the inside and outside walls before we nailed on the boards—so the sawdust won't fall through the cracks!"

"I can't wait to tell Father I know what his insulation is," Martha chuckled.

Raymond helped to finish loading the slabs and then they were on their way to the building site.

Putt, putt, putt, the tractor labored, pulling the shaky load.

"Watch out!" Martha hollered as a slab slid, almost skinning her leg.

It was noon by the time they finished unloading the slabs.

"We should eat dinner even though Father isn't here," Mother decided when the children entered the house.

"Guess what we found out this morning," Martha challenged Mother.

"That might be hard to guess," Mother smiled.

"We discovered what Father plans to use for insulation—or at least we think we did."

"You mean you discovered," Raymond corrected Martha.

"Well, Linda asked a question that gave me the idea," Martha explained, "so it wasn't all me."

"What is he going to use?" Mother questioned with a wise look.

"Sawdust!" Martha announced.

"You're right, "Mother smiled in agreement. "That's why Father and I were so thankful God gave us warm, sunny days for the past week. The sawdust needed to dry from the last rain. Father checked it yesterday and said it is completely dry, so

*Mother, Martha, and Raymond shoveled sawdust on-
to the wagon.*

he is anxious to get it into the new house before another rain."

At the dinner table Mother suddenly exclaimed, "I know what we can do! Let's start loading the wagon with sawdust and surprise Father. Then after he's finished eating, we will be able to start filling the walls."

Mother, Martha, and Raymond went to fill the wagon while Linda and Rodney began to wash the dishes. The job was quickly done, and they waited impatiently for Father to come home and eat.

At last he arrived and after telling him where Mother and the rest were, Rodney and Linda ran down to the sawmill to watch the activity.

"So you guessed my puzzle?" Father smiled to Martha, when he joined them. "And you have the wagon loaded already! Thank you!" he smiled his appreciation to Mother and the children.

Scrambling on top of the load, the children rode to the new building on the sawdust. Raymond drove the tractor, and Mother and Father walked.

Raymond parked the wagon below the

attic door; then, grabbing shovels, he and Father threw the sawdust up into the attic. The walls were easy to fill as Father had left a space open below the plate for the purpose. Later, when the sawdust settled, he would be able to add more as it was needed.

"We need more help," Father said as he paused to rest. "Someone should be filling the wagon again while Raymond and I shovel the sawdust into the walls. The job is too hard for you and the girls," Father told Mother. "I believe I will see if I can get more help."

Before long, Father returned with David, and soon Jonathan, their minister's son, arrived with another tractor and wagon. Now one wagon could be filled with sawdust while the other was being unloaded. The crew worked busily through the long evening.

The next morning Father was surprised when a truck drove in with three brethren. "Brother Wayne spread the word around about your project, so we are here to help," Brother Jim told Father as he took a shovel from the back of the truck.

All day the men loaded and unloaded sawdust. By evening the walls of the new house were filled, and a thick layer of sawdust had been spread over the attic floor. Only the walls below the windows were not finished. Father would do that the next day.

As the weary but grateful family gathered around the supper table, Father prayed sincerely, thanking God for the Christian brethren who cared for others and unselfishly sacrificed their time to help them.

"Bear ye one another's burdens, and so fulful the law of Christ" (Galatians 6:2).

21

Disappointments

Plop, plop, plop. Mother picked the first sweet, tender peas and dropped them into a bucket. August had arrived, and with it the garden vegetables were ripening, ready to can.

How pleasant the cool morning air was and how peaceful to be working alone in the quiet garden with only the sounds of nature around.

Mother's thoughts turned to God. How wonderfully He had planned everything! The busiest days of building the new house were over. Now they would have time to can their garden harvest for winter use.

A car drove slowly past, breaking the silence. Mother started humming as her fingers flew among the pea vines, seeking out the plump tight pods.

"Mother, Mother! Come quickly!" Linda called breathlessly as she burst through the garden gate at top speed. "A man wants to talk to you."

Quickly Mother stood up, then hurried to the house.

"I'm a representative from the Northern Power Company," the man said as he showed Mother his card. "We are going to build a power line starting at your local town and running ten miles this way. Your only cost is what footage we would have to cover from the road to your farm."

For several minutes he talked on, telling Mother of the many advantages having electricity would offer. "Take these papers," he said, handing them to Mother. "Show them to your husband, and I will stop back later today. Your farm is close to the road, and depending where you want your line to be, it wouldn't be that expensive."

Mother had listened quietly while he

talked, and now she thanked him. "I will show these to my husband, then you can discuss it with him," she told the man.

When he had left, the children crowded around Mother, all excited. "Do you think we'll get power?" Rodney asked, his eyes shining.

"Just think!" Martha added. "We wouldn't have to do so much canning. We could have a deepfreeze—and even a refrigerator and stove like Genes have in town."

"Now don't get your hopes up," Mother told the children. "It will depend on how much it costs us to bring it to the farm. I'm sure, though, we won't be buying stoves or refrigerators for a long time. We better not plan on getting electricity," she told them kindly, "so we won't be disappointed if Father decides we'll not be getting it at this time."

Later that afternoon the same man returned, and this time he talked with Father. For a long time they stood talking and figuring.

"See them looking at the side of the house," Linda whispered to Rodney as she peeked out the window. "I think we'll probably get it."

"Mother doesn't think so," Martha said. "At least not this year."

Disappointedly Linda turned back to her dish of unshelled peas. *Snap, snap.* Slowly she shelled while her dreams of turning on electric lights vanished.

"Are we getting electricity?" Rodney asked as soon as Father stepped inside the kitchen.

"Not so fast, Son. Mother and I haven't talked it over yet. We'll tell you as soon as we decide. Right now I need a strong man out at the barn."

Rodney smiled at Father and hurried to keep up with his long strides as they left for the barn.

"I wonder how Raymond and David are coming on their shack," Martha was thinking aloud.

"Let's go see," Linda suggested eagerly. "We're almost done shelling." Now her hands flew. *Snap, snap, snap;* the peas popped into her dish. "May we go, Mother?"

"There will probably be time," Mother consented, "as soon as the peas are washed and packed into jars."

"You can carry out the shells and sweep the floor," Mother told Linda as Martha dumped some peas into a pan of water for washing. "Then when the peas are ready you can help fill jars."

How pretty the full jars of green peas looked as the rows on the cupboard grew longer. Linda could hardly wait to taste the delicious, fresh, cooked peas she knew they were having for supper.

Finally the girls were free. As they neared the edge of the forest they could hear the boys busily hammering away.

"Ya-hoo!" Martha hollered. "Raymond!"

The hammering quit and Raymond called back, "We're over here."

The girls could soon see the slab walls of the boys' shack. "You've really been working!" Martha exclaimed in admiration.

Pleased, Raymond showed the girls the nearly finished walls and the slabs that were the start of the roof.

"O Raymond, I think the spot you have picked is just perfect!" Martha declared softly. Deep soft moss made up the flooring in the little slab house while overhead the sweeping pine branches seemed to shelter it. The area beneath the trees was nearly free of underbrush, so it was easy to walk under the towering pines.

"Will we be able to come out here whenever we want to?" Martha questioned Raymond.

"If David doesn't mind."

"I guess," David offered generously. "But make sure you always give a warning call like today. We don't want to think a moose or bear is about ready to charge in," he said, laughing.

Linda shivered. She knew one thing: she would not be coming by herself no matter how much she loved being in the woods.

Several days later Mother and the girls were again in the garden. This time they were picking the first green beans. Disappointedly they listened while Mother told them that Father and she decided not to have the power line brought to their farm.

"Why?" Martha asked. "Why do others always seem to get what they need, and we don't? We need electricity, too."

Slowly Mother picked a few more beans

before looking into Martha's troubled eyes. "Martha," she said softly, "God wants us to be content with what we have. Father would like to wait until we harvest our crops, and if God blesses us materially, then maybe we will be able to have electricity put in. But if not, maybe it will be possible the next year.

"Let's not fret and wish. That only brings discontentment. Many, many disappointments come to us in a lifetime, but if we praise God and willingly submit, we will be blessed of God and always be happy."

Silently they continued picking beans. Finally Martha broke the silence. "I'm sorry, Mother. It's—it's just that it seems we often have to do without. I guess I thought this would be something we would surely be able to have."

Linda had listened soberly to Mother and Martha. She, too, was disappointed, but Mother had explained things so well, she was content.

"I think we should stop a moment and have a prayer meeting right in the garden," Mother said softly, "asking God to help us each to be content."

The garden became a hallowed spot as

Mother and her daughters prayed, asking God for grace to accept what came their way. A great peace came to Martha. Her heart was full of love for her Mother who so kindly and gently helped them overcome their problems.

A bird chirped, singing from its perch on the raspberry bushes. Sweetly its notes drifted over the garden as Martha returned Mother's smile.

The garden became a hallowed spot.

"Not that I speak in respect of want: for I have learned, in whatsoever state I am, therewith to be content" (Philippians 4:11).

"And be content with such things as ye have: for he hath said, I will never leave thee, nor forsake thee" (Hebrews 13:5).

22

Hailstorm

"It's so hot today," Linda complained as she flopped down on the nearest chair. "If only there would be a breeze."

"I know, Dear, but complaining won't help." Then after a moment Mother asked kindly, "Did you forget your Sunday school lesson already?" She reached into the woodbox for some wood and put it into the cookstove.

It was bread-baking day. If it was hot outside, it was even hotter inside since the fire had to be kept going so the oven would be hot enough to bake the bread.

"I guess," Linda mumbled.

It *was* hot in the kitchen, and Mother and Martha had been busy all afternoon working there. Whenever it was bread-baking day, they baked other things, too. Linda was ashamed as she watched Mother wipe beads of perspiration from her forehead. Here she was not even helping and she was the one who was complaining.

Then she noticed the almost-empty water bucket sitting by the cupboard. Quickly she picked it up and hurried out the door. As she pumped water she thought about what they had discussed in Sunday school. Their memory verse had been Ephesians 5:20: "Giving thanks always for all things unto God and the Father in the name of our Lord Jesus Christ." Sister Anna had explained that that meant for every little thing—even the things that did not go as we wanted them to, or thought they should.

Linda's bucket was full, and she let the last of the water trickle over her bare feet. It felt coolly refreshing. Somehow it did not seem quite as hot anymore.

Linda softly entered the kitchen and silently set the bucket in its place.

"Thank you, Linda," Mother spoke as she took a pan of cookies from the oven. "You may check the water in the stove and if it's hot enough, the baking dishes could be washed. Then there won't be so many dishes to wash at supper time."

The wood cookstove had a reservoir along one end which provided the convenience of an almost constant supply of hot water. Linda picked up the dipper that hung beside the stove and filled the dishpans. Then she refilled the reservoir with cold water so there would be hot water ready for the next person who needed some. Humming softly, Linda swished the soap round and round, making suds.

"Have you been thinking of your Sunday school lesson?" Mother asked kindly. "It is much more pleasant to hear you humming than complaining. We have a wonderful privilege of being able to learn what God expects of us from ministers, parents, and teachers. We must do our part and be willing to obey."

Linda nodded with a smile. "I don't seem to feel nearly as hot now, either," she added, "and I'm even washing dishes in hot water!"

"That's because you are willing to help and are doing it cheerfully," Mother replied. "When we do something to help someone else, we receive a greater joy than when we do things to please ourselves."

Bang—the screen door slammed and Raymond rushed in. "It's going to storm. You should see the funny black clouds in the sky."

Mother and the girls hurried outdoors. The sky in the southwest was filled with dark clouds that seemed to churn and boil as they swiftly rolled closer to the farm.

"Run and pen up the chickens," Mother instructed Raymond quickly. She scanned the field behind the barn. Where were Father and the other children? They had gone to get a load of slabs to use as firewood.

"There they are!" Linda's voice held excitement, and everyone breathed a sigh of relief as the wagon rolled around the corner of the barn.

The wind was starting to blow, and a few raindrops spattered down. Linda watched as Father jumped off the tractor, unhitched the wagon, then drove the tractor into the shed.

Rodney, Joanna, and Donnie, started

running to the house. Raymond, who was just leaving the chicken house, picked up Donnie, grabbed Joanna's hand, and raced with Rodney to the house. They joined Mother and the girls on the porch and waited for Father to come.

Father was struggling with the doors against the wind. He finally fastened them tightly and ran for the house just as the heavens seemed to open and the rain fell in torrents. Together the family entered the house and closed the door against the storm.

"I'm afraid we will get some hail with the wind and rain. It's been so hot and still today."

Father had scarcely spoken the words when *ping, ping, ping, ping,* small hailstones sang against the windows. Then with a loud roar, hail poured down, making the outdoors look as white as a sheet. Not a word was spoken as everyone stood awestruck and surrounded by the deafening noise.

"Quick, the bedroom windows!" Father's shout startled them as he ran for the boys' bedroom windows against which the hail was pounding. Grabbing pillows from the bed, Father rammed them up against the glass.

Mother hurriedly jerked off the top blanket and held it tightly against the glass in the other window.

"Raymond and Martha, help us," Father shouted.

Wide-eyed, the younger children watched and listened as the hail pounded on the roof over the unceiled bedroom. It seemed it would never stop.

But as suddenly as the storm had started, it stopped. The silence seemed strange and unreal. The pillows and blanket were taken down from the windows; even with the padded protection they had afforded, one window had been broken.

Now they could see the effects of the storm. Hail, leaves, and branches were scattered everywhere in a heavy layer. It was piled in drifts against the buildings.

"Let's go outside," Father spoke quietly.

"Look at the size of these hailstones!" Raymond exclaimed as he picked one up. It was a good inch in diameter.

"No wonder the sound was so deafening," Mother spoke softly. "How thankful we can be that the chickens and cattle were all safely under cover."

"I guess that takes care of our threshing, too," Father added.

The children's eyes followed Father's as he looked across the road to the field where the oats had stood with tops bowed over, heavy with grain. They saw nothing. The oats had been completely flattened by the hail.

"O Father, what will we do?" Raymond asked anxiously. "How will we feed our cows this winter?"

"Son," Father rebuked him gently, "remember, our trust is in God, not in earthly possessions. There is no need for us to fret or worry. God knows our needs, and He will supply every one if we put our trust in Him. It may not be according to our plans and wants, but God has promised to supply our needs. If we ask God and have faith, He will answer.

"This experience shows us how helpless we really are. We can work hard from morning until evening, but it is God who sends us the rain and sunshine and makes the crops grow. He also sends us the storms. Maybe we needed this storm to draw us closer to God, to help us realize we must depend on God and not on ourselves."

The sun was shining again, and the warmth felt good in contrast to the coldness of the hailstones.

"Could we make ice cream?" Father looked questioningly at Mother. "With the sun shining, the hail will soon melt."

"Yes," she answered smiling. "it will make a nice treat for all of us."

Father started toward the barn to get the shovel, while Mother went into the house. Linda stooped to pick up a hailstone, then popped it into her mouth. She had not tasted the coldness of ice since last winter, and it was good. Then she remembered again what her Sunday school teacher had said about giving thanks always for all things.

"And that's just what Father did!" she exclaimed aloud.

"O Father, You have taken all
With hail You sent our way;
The crops and gardens beaten down,
What shall we do?" we pray.

"Your Word, it says to take no thought
Of what the morrow brings;
But I am weary from unrest,
My heart no longer sings."

"My child, come closer now to Me,
I will your burdens bear.
For as you put your trust in Me,
You will be in My care."

"I'm sorry, Father!" then I cried
As tears did freely flow,
Cleansing my heart from unbelief—
What peace I then did know.

With joyful heart I raised my head,
My lips burst forth in song!
For would not God in heaven care
For me the whole day long?

23

Learning God's Care

How beaten and ragged the poor garden looked after the storm. The rows and rows of peas, beans, corn, and tomatoes lay battered and broken. Tears of rebellion came to Martha's eyes and her heart demanded, "Why? Why? Why this?"

For a long time Martha stood silently surveying the ruins while a battle raged in her heart. "O Father in heaven," she quietly prayed, "help me to understand."

Martha knew that this same rebellion often stayed with her for days before she had given her heart to the Lord. Now, as a child of God, she desperately wanted to overcome her resentment against God.

In the stillness of the garden, the Spirit gently brought some verses from Matthew to her mind: "Take therefore no thought for the morrow: for the morrow shall take thought for the things of itself." And, "Therefore take no thought, saying, What shall we eat? or, What shall we drink? or, Wherewithal shall we be clothed?" (Matthew 6:34 and 31).

A calmness stole over Martha's heart. She bowed her head and breathed a thank you to God for reminding her of His faithfulness.

Martha walked back toward the house. "It's just like Mother says," she thought as she remembered Mother's words: "God's children are safe in His care."

Quietly Martha entered the new house and watched as Father hammered away, putting up partitions. The room dividers were giving it the appearance of a house.

"How are our beds going to fit into the bedrooms?" she asked, puzzled as she noticed the smallness of the rooms.

"I'll show you," Father offered with a smile as he laid his hammer down. "We're planning to make double bunk beds for your room and the boys. Then I'll put corner shelves in each room to take the place of dressers.''

"That sounds cozy! I'm getting eager to move in," Martha answered. "I guess I should have known you would have everything figured out!''

Father returned her smile. "By the way, I have a job you could do. Will you come with me?" Martha followed Father as he headed for the shop. "Would you please wash these windows?" he asked, pointing to a stack of dirty, cobwebby windows.

"Yes, I'll be glad to, but where did you get them?" Martha wondered.

"From an old, old chicken house that used to be on this farm. I've been saving them for something, sometime.''

"Trust Father," Martha thought as she helped to carry the windows outside. "He can always make something out of nothing." Mentally she counted the windows. One for each bedroom, one for the living room, and three for above the cupboards. Sure enough, there were exactly the right amount.

"Did you plan the number of windows

you were going to put in the house according to the number of windows that are here?'' she asked.

"Yes, I did,'' Father replied with a twinkle in his eye. "Now let's surprise Mother. She's been wondering what we are going to do for windows.''

Enthusiastically, Martha set about her task, eager to help.

That afternoon David and Raymond met at their shack. They looked in dismay at the damage the storm had done. The top of one of the pines had been snapped off and had fallen on the roof, smashing it and knocking one of the walls down. Crestfallen they stood looking at the ruins, thinking of all the work, time, and anticipation they had put into the project.

"We were almost finished,'' David finally broke the painful silence. "Now what?'' Questioningly he looked at Raymond.

Raymond kicked at a broken board. "Guess we'll just have to forget it,'' he answered dejectedly. "There's only a couple more weeks until school starts anyway, so we hardly have time to fix it up again.''

"I guess,'' David agreed.

"We were almost finished." David finally broke the painful silence.

Since there was nothing for them to do, the boys soon parted, each lost in his own discouraged thoughts.

Raymond had only walked a short distance when David called after him. "Just a minute. I want to talk to you."

Raymond waited while David hurried back to him. "Do you think that maybe next summer we could tear the roof off and fix the wall that is broken down?"

"Maybe we could." Raymond brightened at the thought. "We have worked so hard on our shack."

"At least we can think about it," David added. "Well, see you later," he called as they parted—this time in better spirits.

After Raymond reported to his family what had happened to the shack, Father spoke encouragingly. "It might be possible for me to help you fix it up later this fall, or maybe in the spring. Not all is lost, and repairing it the second time won't take as long as building it in the first place did."

"Thanks, Father," Raymond replied gratefully.

By the end of that week, Father had all the rooms in the new house partitioned off and was putting in the windows.

"Go and tell Mother I would like her to come out here if she could," Father instructed Rodney. He placed the last of the windows in position and stood back to observe the effect. Satisfied, he picked up his tools and went into the bedroom.

"Father wants you at the new house," Rodney told Mother, breathless from his run.

Mother laid down her sewing and followed Rodney outside. Martha, thinking she knew why Father wanted Mother, quietly slipped from the house and followed. She wanted to see Mother's reaction.

When Mother entered the building, Father was nowhere in sight. "John!" Mother called. "John, where are you?" Then Mother's mouth dropped open in surprise as she noticed the clean, sparkling windows in their places. "What . . . !"

Father came from the bedroom with a big smile on his face. "Are you satisfied?" he asked Mother.

"Satisfied? O John, yes! It looks like a home already. It hardly seems real that we were able to build this house with it costing hardly anything," Mother answered, her voice full of emotion.

Turning, Martha—who had watched from the doorway and enjoyed Mother's surprise—slipped away unnoticed. She had a lump in her throat, one of happiness and love.

The next day Father drove along to town with Brother Wayne. When he arrived home, he handed a letter to Mother. "I would like you to read this right now," he said.

When she had finished, Mother silently handed the letter back to Father, blinking back sudden tears.

"Our God answers prayer," Father said quietly. "We have made out fine with the tractor this summer, but winter will soon be coming."

Later that evening Father told the children who listened in wonderment, "Uncle Verns wrote that they and some other of our relatives want to purchase a van for us. We have all been praying about this need, children, and God has marvelously answered. Let us thank Him now."

Together the family knelt and each one thanked God for the promised vehicle. Father closed, "Dear Father in heaven, we thank

Thee for Thy goodness to us and for answering our prayers. Make us worthy of this gift, by Thy grace, and give us wisdom to use it to bring honor and glory to Thy Name. May we remember that it has come as a gift from Thy hand, and may it be used accordingly. Bless and reward our dear brethren who are willing to serve others in love for Thy sake. We thank Thee for Thy promised, never-failing love and care. In Jesus' Name. Amen."

24

Visiting Bush Mill

The summer days were rapidly slipping by. Gradually the nights were becoming cooler. No longer could you slip outdoors in the early morning stillness without a sweater or jacket, and the warmth of the wood cook stove was welcome. However, by midmorning, the sun's rays shone so warmly that the thought of a sweater or coat was entirely forgotten.

One August morning the family was seated at the table enjoying Mother's good hot breakfast of cereal and muffins. "Would it suit you to come out to the bush sawmill today?'' Father questioned Mother. He reached for another muffin, spreading it with good, homemade butter.

"Yes, I believe it would," Mother answered after a few moments of thought.

"Yesterday when we were sawing, I noticed some cranberries. There may not be many because of the hailstorm, but I believe you could find some. The ones I saw were nice and big."

"I would like to have some. Should we bring dinner along and hunt berries all day?" Mother looked at Father, waiting for his answer.

"That sounds fine. Raymond and I will take the little Ford tractor, and you may bring the other tractor with the wagon."

Father and Raymond left promptly for the bush. The house became a beehive of activity. Martha was making the beds and dustmopping the floors. Linda and Rodney were busily washing the dishes at the cupboard. Mother made sandwiches and collected other food items for a lunch. Joanna skipped here and there, asking questions and doing little jobs. Even Donnie helped.

By the time the children had their work

finished, Mother had the dinner packed. Buckets, jackets, scarves, and caps were collected, and then the children found places on the wagon.

"It seems funny to see Mother driving," Linda giggled as they sped along, watching Mother's scarf float out behind her on the breeze.

A few miles down the road, Mother slowed and turned off onto a logging trail that led through the dense forest. Thick underbrush guarded each side of the trail, and tall trees cast dark shadows over the road. Joanna shivered and moved close to Martha, watching everything with big, solemn eyes. They followed this trail for nearly a mile, then turned to the left.

Ahead lay the sawmill. But something was wrong! Raymond sat slumped by a log with his head between his legs. Father was kneeling beside him.

Mother quickly stopped the tractor and hurried to them. The others followed close behind. Wide-eyed they looked at Raymond, who sat white and limp. Blood was spattered on his shirt and hands.

"What happened?" Mother asked Father

anxiously as she knelt beside them. "Is he hurt very badly?"

"No, I don't think so. He got his finger in the blade and almost fainted. Get me some water and something to use for a bandage."

After washing the badly torn finger, Father wrapped it with a clean handkerchief, tying it securely with the hem he had torn from the hanky.

"How are you feeling, Son?" Mother asked when Raymond raised his ashen face.

"I'll be better in a little while," he mumbled weakly. "I don't know how it happened. Guess I wasn't watching."

Turning to Father, Mother offered, "I can help you saw, then you won't need to stop working."

Father agreed, and Mother gave some instructions to the berry pickers.

"You must all stay together," she said. "And, Martha, remember to keep your eye on the younger ones."

"I will," Martha promised, and the children started off.

"Just look at the cranberries!" Linda exclaimed when they came to a large open space in the woods where low, green plants carpeted the forest floor. Cranberries seemed to be everywhere.

"There are not many berries on a plant," Martha observed, "but at least they are big ones."

Ping, ping, ping—the berries bounced in the children's empty buckets.

Whin-nee—screech—the sawmill buzzed, adding its noise to the gentle *ping, ping* of the berry pickers. Bright sunshine splashed into the clearing, making the day warm and cheery.

Joanna kept close to Martha. Every now and then she cast a quick glance at the foreboding forest that surrounded them.

"Martha," she asked in a whisper, "are there any bears in the trees?"

"No, I don't think so," Martha smiled reassuringly. "The sawmill is so noisy it has probably scared any bears away that might have been near."

Joanna gave a sigh of relief.

Rodney, overhearing the conversation, started laughing. "I wouldn't be afraid if I saw a bear. Raymond said they are so fat this time of the year they can hardly run. All they do is waddle!"

"I know what I would do," Linda joined Rodney laughing. "I would say, 'Hi! Are you looking for berries, too?' "

"Linda, Rodney. Stop," Martha said. "You both know better than to boast like that."

As Linda continued to pick berries, she recalled guiltily her resolution never to go to Raymond's shack alone. "Oh, well," she excused herself, "there are no bears around here anyway."

Martha had begun to fill her second bucket, and the gallon buckets the others were using were nearly full, when Father shut the tractor off that ran the saw and called them for dinner.

"We won't do any more sawing today," Father told Mother. "I'll help you pick a few more berries, and then we'll all go home early."

After dinner the cranberry picking went slower. The sun was hot and backs and legs were aching from crouching over.

"These bushes keep scratching me," Linda complained to Rodney. "I'm going to find a better place to pick. Look, Rodney," she called from the edge of the clearing, "there are cranberries here, too."

Rodney hurried to her, and together they continued to pick, wandering from one spot to another, always finding more berries ahead.

"Let's rest," sighed Linda awhile later as she found a place to sit down.

Then Rodney noticed dead, blackened tree trunks protruding from clumps of young trees. "Linda, where are we?" he asked in a scared voice.

Alarmed, Linda glanced about, looking for some sign of the others. But everything was silent.

Snap! Crack! Crack-crack!

Terrified, Linda and Rodney whirled around to see a huge black bear as he rose up on his hind paws not far away.

Linda and Rodney's legs seemed to turn to rubber as they stood dazed, unable to think or move. The bear lifted a paw slowly and Linda let out a scream. Grabbing Rodney's hand, she turned and fled. Blindly and frantically the children crashed and stumbled through the underbrush, their only thought being to get away from the bear.

Before they reached the clearing where

the rest of the family were picking, they met Father racing toward them.

"Bear!" Linda and Rodney sobbed, clinging to Father.

But there was no sign of a bear.

"By the sounds of your screams, you probably chased him in the opposite direction," Raymond chuckled.

Father had to smile at Raymond's supposition, but heartily agreed. Realizing that the bear probably had not even followed them made Linda feel foolish.

"Did you forget your boastful plans?" Martha quietly asked Linda.

"What do you mean?" questioned Father.

Martha explained how when Joanna had been afraid that there were bears around, Rodney had said he would not be afraid of a bear and how Linda had laughed and said she would just say, "Hi! Are you looking for berries, too?"

Raymond burst out laughing. Even Father and Mother could not keep from chuckling when they thought of Rodney and Linda's bravado and of what had actually happened.

"It's different," Rodney admitted with a shaky laugh, "when you actually see one."

Linda meekly set her empty bucket on the wagon and climbed up beside it. No longer did she feel so bold and fearless.

25

Fire!

"A school bus! Father is going to drive our public school bus this year!" Excitedly the children talked among themselves.

What fun it was to help clean the bus when Father brought it home. It was even more fun to sit in the big, high seats when they had finished cleaning it and pretend they were on a trip to some faraway place.

School started, and with it came the change of getting out of bed early in the morning so the chores could be finished before Father left to pick up the school children. It seemed strange to be at home only in the evenings, but after the first week, they had gotten used to the idea of going to school each day.

One morning during the second week Raymond looked anxiously around the living room. "Has anyone seen my math book? I'm sure I left it on the bookshelf last night."

"Try looking by the couch," Mother replied from the kitchen. "You were doing your homework there before bedtime." Mother stopped washing dishes and continued, "Don't you think you are becoming careless with your belongings? I'm sure it would be less frustrating for you if you would put things away when you are finished with them."

Raymond hurried to the couch. There was his math book lying on the floor. As he picked it up, he glanced out the nearby window. What he saw made him stand and stare. Their neighbor's truck was flying down the hill. As it neared their lane, with brakes screeching, the truck turned in and came tearing up towards the house.

"Mother, Ted Lane is here and I think something is wrong." Raymond called to Mother as he headed for the door.

The truck flew toward the chicken house, drove behind it and stopped.

"Martha and Linda, please stay in the house with the younger children," Mother instructed. "Raymond, I want you to come with me."

Mother and Raymond hurried outside as Mr. Lane started his truck again and headed for the house. On the back of his truck was their long ladder.

"Quick! Your house roof is on fire!" he shouted as he jumped from the truck. "I'll need buckets of water."

Dragging the ladder off his truck, Mr. Lane ran for the house.

"Raymond! Hurry! The milk buckets are still in the house," Mother instructed as she ran for the water pump and began pumping.

It seemed to take forever for the water to come. Up and down, up and down; she pumped as fast as she could. With a prayer of thanksgiving, she watched the water come gushing out.

Grabbing both pails, Mother filled one. Then shoving the second pail under the water spout, she panted to Raymond, "Keep pumping. I'll get Martha to pump so you can carry water."

By the time the second pail was full, Mother and Martha were back bringing a third bucket with them. Martha began to pump and Raymond ran with the full bucket.

Up, down; up, down. Martha tried to think of how much she was helping instead of thinking of her aching arms.

Up, down; up, down. She was so busy pumping water she had not even had time to see the fire.

Up, down; up, down. Backing up a few steps she took a quick glance at the roof. The shingles had burned around the chimney, and the fire had spread to both sides of the roof.

"Martha!" Mother startled her. "You'll have to keep pumping."

Up, down; up, down. Up, down; up, down.

Just then Father slowed the school bus down at the end of the lane. He came panting toward the pump. "Mother, take the school bus to school. I'll stay here and help put out the fire."

Linda and the younger children had clustered around the kitchen window, watching the excitement outside. As Linda saw Mother climb into the school bus and

Up, down; up, down. Martha's arms ached.

start driving away, she said, "Rodney, you, Joanna, and Donnie stay right here by the window. I'm going outside to see what is going on and you must not come. You would only get in the way."

"But Mother said you are supposed to stay in here," Rodney frowned.

"I'll be back pretty soon. Now don't you move," Linda commanded sternly as she guiltily slipped out the door.

As soon as Linda had gone, Donnie started crying. Then Joanna asked in a frightened voice, "What's all that noise?"

Thump, thump, thump, sounded overhead. Then water started dripping from the ceiling and onto the table and floor.

"Maybe the roof is going to fall down on us," Rodney burst out tearfully.

Joanna, thoroughly frightened now, burst into tears.

At this point, Father opened the door. "What's the matter?" Father asked kindly. "Where's Linda?"

"She told us to stay right here, and then she went outside," Joanna sobbed. "We thought the roof was going to fall on us."

"Water, water," Donnie lisped as he

crowded close to Father.

Father picked up Donnie and then explained gently, "The water dripping down is from the water Ted and I dashed on the fire to put it out. The fire burned away some shingles, so that's why the roof is leaking. If there had been any real danger to you children, we would have taken you out of the house."

"But what was banging around?" Rodney wondered, wide-eyed.

"That was Ted and I walking on the roof, Son."

Bang. The door slammed as Martha, Raymond, and Linda came inside.

"It sure was a good thing Ted Lane happened to be driving by," Raymond talked excitedly. "If he wouldn't have come when he did, we wouldn't have known about the fire until we walked down the lane to meet the school bus. Maybe a lot more of the roof would have burned."

"No, Raymond," Father interrupted. "Ted Lane didn't just happen to be driving by. God has control of our lives. God protected us and our home by sending Ted Lane at the time we needed him. God sees us all the time and knows what we are doing, what we need, and even what we are thinking. Let's remember, children, that God is caring for us.

"Then, too," Father continued, "Ted Lane is probably the only neighbor who knows where we keep our ladders. God knew this, too, as He knows every other detail of our lives. Rodney, please bring me my Bible." Father pulled out a chair by the table and sat down. "I want to show you children some verses in Matthew."

Rodney quickly brought Father's Bible, and everyone crowded close as Father turned the pages.

"Martha, will you please read verses 29 through 31 of chapter 10?"

Slowly Martha read, " 'Are not two sparrows sold for a farthing? and one of them shall not fall on the ground without your Father. But the very hairs of your head are all numbered. Fear ye not therefore, ye are of more value than many sparrows.' "

"I know now what you mean, Father, about Ted Lane not just happening to come by," Raymond nodded soberly. "If God knows how many hairs I have on my head, surely He knows everything."

"And aren't we thankful?" Father questioned as he smiled at the children.

"Yes," they chorused.

The hum of the school bus could be heard as Mother came up the lane. Eagerly the children ran to meet her. Father followed, carrying Donnie. Everyone tried to talk at once, there was so much to tell Mother. Mother listened to their excited chatter, and then she suggested they show the younger children where the fire had been.

Walking around to the side of the house, they could see a large, blackened area around the chimney where the fire had burned away the wooden shingles.

Joanna silently slipped her hand into Mother's and shyly whispered, "Mother, I was afraid when Linda left us in the house all alone."

Linda, who was standing near enough to hear, hung her head as Mother looked at her. "I'm sorry," she said meekly. "I know I should have taken care of the younger ones. But—but it was so hard to stay inside and not know what was going on. Then I kind of forgot about them," she added, ashamed.

SAFE IN HIS CARE

"I'm glad you are sorry, but you were disobedient. You must learn to patiently do whatever duty you are given to do, even if the task seems unpleasant or unimportant." Mother looked sadly at Linda. "Father and I want to be able to trust you. The younger children are watching you, too, and taking you for an example, whether it be good or bad," Mother told her.

Tears came to Linda's eyes at Mother's grieved look. "Mother, I am truly sorry. I want to be dependable so you and Father can trust me. And I want to be a good example to the younger ones. God will help me," she added as the tears fell.

"Yes, Linda, He will. Always look to Him for the grace to do what is right. He will give it to you. You are forgiven. Dry your tears now. I see Father and Raymond have gone to the shop. They will probably start fixing the roof. Since there will be no school for you children today, you can help me in the house."

Together Mother and the girls started cleaning up the mess inside. As they worked, the girls told Mother about the verses Father had shown them.

"Just think," Linda exclaimed, "God even knows how many hairs I have!"

"Yes, and God sees us right at this moment and knows everything about us," Mother added softly.

26

Lodgers

With the first fall frost, the hillsides were splashed with bright color, though they were not as colorful as usual because the hailstorm had stripped off many leaves. They were pretty, nevertheless, with the brilliancy of many colors dappled among the dark evergreens.

The usual bustle of harvest was lacking, for the hailstorm had already threshed the oats. Father and Raymond were raking the flattened grain field, saving the straw and what grain they could salvage as feed for the cattle.

Rodney, Joanna, and Linda loved to watch the rake gather the straw together, making long, thin rows around the field. When their Saturday's work was finished, the three headed for the wooden fence that separated the grain field from the sheep corrals. Teetering on its top, they gaily tried to see who could walk the farthest without falling off.

"Oh, ouch! My knee!" Joanna wailed when she slipped off the rail, skinning her knee.

Linda quickly jumped from the fence beside Joanna. "It's not skinned too badly," she comforted. "See, your stocking isn't even torn. Let's rest awhile."

The three sat at the edge of the oats field and watched the tractor and rake come their way with spinning wheels gathering up the loose straw. Raymond waved as he turned the corner and started back across the field.

Busy school days came and passed swiftly. Each night the moon was getting bigger and brighter, and the days became colder.

"We're going to have a hard killing frost over full moon, and our winter snows will soon be coming," Father announced at the breakfast table one morning. "That means we must get our potatoes dug. Mother and I have decided everyone will stay home from school today and help dig them."

Coats, hats, boots, and mitts were found and donned, and Father and the older children left the warm house for the chilly outdoors. A light frost covered the ground, and their boots *crunch, crunched* as they hurried down the path to the garden. Soon potatoes were *thud, thud, thudding* into empty buckets.

"It's cold this morning." Linda's teeth chattered as she stopped to rest.

"You will have to work faster so you can keep warm," Martha teased as she emptied her full bucket into an empty gunny sack. "Let me hold the sack for you," she added. "It's hard to do it alone. And if you and Rodney keep up with me, I'll help you every time," she kindly offered.

By dinner time the last of the potatoes had been put into gunny sacks. Weary, cold, and hungry, they trudged to the house for dinner.

"I'm glad that job is finished," Linda

sighed as she sat down to the table.

"Yes. So am I." Father's eyes twinkled as he spoke. "The Lord has given us a good potato crop, considering the hailstorm. And I had a crew of diligent helpers this morning to harvest the crop. Thank you, everyone."

Linda felt a happy glow inside. She smiled at Rodney. It had been worth the effort to keep up with the older ones. She was very tired, but that did not matter.

In the late afternoon, the first snowflakes sifted down from the gray, overcast sky. Father had finished plowing the garden, and it was beginning to get dark when Raymond helped him bend the tops of the raspberry bushes to the ground and lay poles on them to hold them down. The winter snows would soon cover them, keeping them from being eaten by the rabbits, and they would have raspberries again next summer.

When that job was finished, Father brought the potatoes to the house on the wagon and carried the heavy sacks to the cellar where Raymond helped him fill the bins.

"It is nice to see the potato bins full," Raymond said as he looked at the half-empty canned goods shelves, a reminder that the hail-beaten garden had produced poorly. "And we can be thankful we all like red beet pickles," he grinned, looking at the rows and rows of red.

"Yes, Son, this winter we'll be glad Mother canned so many," Father answered. "We may not have a large variety of food, but I'm sure we will not go hungry."

As Raymond climbed the cellar ladder, he remembered that Father had said there was no need to worry because God knew their need. With a light heart, he put the cellar door back into place. "God is already providing through Father's bus job," he thought. "Some way there will be enough food for the animals and anything else we need."

One evening as the school children stepped off the bus, they were surprised to see a small wooden house on wheels parked in their yard. Excitedly they raced for the house.

"Sh!" Mother met them at the door, her finger to her lips. "Don't wake Donnie. First, take off your coats and boots, then I will tell you about the little house.

"God is continuing to supply our needs," Mother began as the children gathered around her. "Do you remember the hailstorm and how it flattened our crops and garden? Father and I have been praying about it and asking God to provide as He sees best. The little house out there is a bunk house and belongs to four men who are working for the government. These men are going to be clearing trees and brush and need a place to park their trailer. Also, they need someone to cook for them. They will pay us. Children, never forget that God is providing wonderfully," Mother added, her voice filled with emotion.

27

Surprises

"We're moving, we're moving!" Joanna chanted, skipping from one room to another.

Already the house had an empty appearance. Quite a few items had been carried over to the new home. The curtainless windows in the old house made it seem bare and cold. Father had just taken the cook stove over and had now returned for the cupboard.

"When may Rodney and I go over to our new house?" Joanna asked eagerly.

"Just wait until we have moved a few more pieces of the bigger furniture," Father told her kindly. "You will help us by staying here out of the way."

Joanna watched as the cupboard was carried out and loaded onto the waiting stoneboat. Soon she was skipping from room to room; once more singing her chant, "We're moving, we're moving!"

"Joanna! Rodney!" Linda's call echoed through the house. "Father said you may come now."

Joanna jumped around so excitedly that Linda could hardly zip up her jacket. Together the three raced over to the new house.

"Welcome home!" Mother called cheerily from the cupboard where she was putting dishes away. "How do you like our home?"

"I'm going to love it," Linda answered contentedly.

"Me, too," Joanna echoed.

"Come see our bedroom," Linda invited, leading the way.

Just inside, behind the door, were the bunk beds Father had made. "Guess where we get to sleep, Joanna." Linda's eyes twinkled.

"Up on top?" Hopefully Joanna waited,

her eyes shining with eager desire.

"You guessed right," Linda smiled. "Look how Father put a rail around the sides and even a ladder."

"I wish it was night time already," Joanna chattered, climbing to the top of the ladder.

That evening the family sat down for supper in their new home. What fun it was washing dishes afterward and sweeping the smooth concrete floor.

"Now we will be ready to start cooking for the men," Mother remarked to Father as she rocked Donnie contentedly.

"We aren't quite ready," Father answered. "There's one thing that needs to be done yet."

"What is that?" Mother asked. "I wasn't aware of anything."

"I think we should have electricity put in before you take on the cooking job."

When Mother did not answer, Father continued, "Since I have the bus driving job and the government men have offered me a job operating a bulldozer, I think we can do it now."

"It would be nice to have," Mother

answered slowly, "but I'm satisfied without it."

"Yes, I know you are. But if you don't object, I am ready to get electricity. I believe God has made us able."

"Whatever you decide, John, will be all right with me." Mother smiled her consent.

"Tomorrow I'll go and see about it." Father yawned. "Right now it's bedtime."

Mother laid the sleeping Donnie on his bed. "Come," she called the children, "it is past bedtime."

"Let us have prayer together before we retire this first night in our new home," Father directed.

The family knelt together and Father prayed a prayer of praise and thanksgiving.

Sleep seemed far away, for the thrill of sleeping in their new, snug house kept the children awake for a long time. No creaking or groaning of old, loose timbers could be heard; only the steady *tick-tock, tick-tock* of the clock and the occasional snapping of the fire greeted their ears as, one by one, they drifted off to sleep.

By the end of the week, an electric line ran from the road to the new house. A few days later Father pulled into the lane, driving Brother Wayne's truck. Puzzled, Mother watched as he backed close to the door. Then her eyes opened in surprised disbelief as she saw a big crate and recognized what was in it.

When Father entered the house, he looked almost guilty.

"Now what have you done?" Mother's words were a teasing exclamation.

There was no creaking and groaning of old, loose timbers in the new, snug house.

"Done?" Father asked innocently. "Well, if you don't like it, we could send it back!"

"A deepfreeze!" Mother could hardly believe what she saw. "When did you order that?"

"A week ago. This is something I want you to have with all the extra cooking work you will be doing."

"Thank you," Mother said softly. "It's a wonderful surprise! I'm sure having a deepfreeze will make it easier."

"I knew we would be butchering soon," Father reminded her. "It will take more meat with the extra men here."

"It is hard to believe," Martha told Mother after her return from school when she saw the gleaming white deepfreeze. "A new house, electricity, a van to come, and now a deepfreeze!"

"Yes, I agree with you," Mother said. "God is good." Lovingly she looked around at their new home. She could see only rough-sawed lumber on the walls and ceiling, with concrete for the floor. But behind it she saw the hard labors of each one in the family. She thought of the long, hard hours the children had worked without complaining, of the planning her husband had done so they could build this house costing little more than the labor of their hands.

"Yes, Martha," Mother repeated, "it is hard to believe. Really, our house was built by the love of each one in our family and now God's love is abundantly supplying our other needs. Our home is very special to me," Mother added quietly.

As Martha pondered Mother's words, she remembered her struggle to submit when the hailstorm struck and her rebellion at having to go to church on a tractor and wagon. And now God was blessing them with even more than they had before! With a heart overflowing with thankfulness, Martha hummed to herself, "I thank the Lord my Maker for all His gifts to me; For making me partaker of bounties rich and free."

28

Without Father

Raymond yawned as he slouched down in his seat, listening to the hum of the school bus tires as they rolled through the darkness. He closed his eyes, letting his mind drift back to his busy day—first school, then helping Father to saw fence posts when he got home, chores, then hurrying to get ready to go to their midweek Bible study after supper. As usual, he was the only boy his age who attended. "If only David would come!" he thought longingly.

He could hear Father and Mother talking up at the front of the bus. The other children were scattered here and there, either sleeping or almost asleep, for the fellowshiping after church had lasted longer than usual.

What was Father saying? Their bishop, Charles Reeder, was coming? Instantly Raymond sat up, wide awake. Intently, he listened.

"The Lord willing, I'll make plans to ride along back with Brother Reeder on Monday. We've made out fine without our own vehicle this fall so far by using the school bus, but I don't like to use it any longer than necessary. The van has been waiting for us for a while, and it looks as though it is working out for me to go and bring it home now."

The van! Raymond had completely forgotten about it with all the excitement of moving, having the power put in, getting the deepfreeze, and the lodgers arriving. He listened again as Father continued talking.

"I'm ahead on the bulldozing, too, so being gone a few days won't inconvenience the men."

Early Monday morning Brother Charles Reeder came for Father. How strange it seemed to eat breakfast and supper with the four boarders without Father being there. When supper was over, the men immediately excused themselves and went outside to their bunkhouse. This was different, for when Father was home they often stayed and questioned him about what he read from the Bible in family devotions.

"What shall we do now?" Linda asked when the dishes had been washed.

"What a long day!" Joanna sighed.

Mother smiled understandingly. "It seems longer because we know Father won't be home tonight. Let me think of something we could do this evening."

"Could we make popcorn?" Martha suggested.

"That does sound good," Mother consented.

"Popcorn, and on a school night!" Rodney exclaimed.

Raymond got up from the couch to add more wood to the stove. Soon the merry crackling of the fire was drowned out by the sound of corn popping.

"It's been a long time since we've had a story," Rodney said wistfully as he tossed a popcorn kernel into his mouth and slowly munched the good, nutty flavor.

"Could you tell one, Mother?" Linda pleaded. "Your stories are always so good."

"Yes, do!" Martha and Raymond encouraged together.

"Sitting around this cozy fire recalls to me a time when God protected one of you," Mother began, lovingly glancing at each of her children.

"Raymond was one-and-a-half years old," Mother began looking at her oldest. "We had moved from Banks three months before and were living at Brother's Wayne's place in an unused granary."

"Banks!" Joanna interrupted, her eyes shining. "You said that is where Father went today."

"Yes, Dear," Mother smiled. "It's the same town where Father will be tonight, the Lord willing."

"Mother used to live there when she was a little girl," Linda informed Joanna.

"Sh-h," Martha whispered. "Let's listen to Mother."

"It was summertime and Raymond would wander all over the barnyard when Brother Wayne was doing chores. Raymond was not afraid of any of the animals, and they didn't seem to be afraid of him, either.

"Father and I did not have a car or truck, but used a two-wheeled cart and horse.

"One day Raymond and I were in the cart ready to go to the neighbor's place. I was checking in my purse to see if I had everything I needed when Raymond pulled himself up at the front of the cart, and before I could grab him he fell over the front, right under the horse's feet.

"Usually when there's an unexpected noise or when something hits a horse, the horse will shy or rear up or even run away because he's been frightened. But our horse stood perfectly still.

"I got out of the cart as fast as I could, and how thankful I was to see Raymond come crawling out from between the horse's feet."

Silently the children munched popcorn, thinking of the story Mother had told.

"God takes care of us so many times," Martha reflected thoughtfully.

"It reminds me of another time when God cared for Raymond," Mother began again. "This happened in the winter when Raymond was three years old. We were living on our own place at this time and were visiting Brother Waynes. He took Raymond outside with him to do chores and needed to draw water from the well for the animals."

"What's drawing water?" Joanna asked, puzzled.

"The well did not have a pump," Mother explained, "so they lowered an empty bucket down into the well, then pulled the full bucket of water up again.

"Remember, I said it was wintertime. Whenever someone would pull up a bucket of water, water would drip from the bucket and sometimes splash out. This would freeze along the sides of the well, making it slippery.

"Brother Wayne told Raymond to stay back so he wouldn't fall into the well, but Raymond was curious to see where the bucket was going. He thought he would take just a little peek, so when Brother Wayne had his back turned and was busy lowering the bucket into the well, Raymond took hold of the well's icy edge and pulled himself up. Before he had time to think what was happening he slipped over the side and started falling down the well.

"Brother Wayne grabbed for Raymond, catching his boot just in time. He brought a sobbing, frightened little boy into the house and told us what had happened. He said he was so badly frightened that the first thing he did after pulling Raymond out was to give him a good spanking.

"Father and I were glad he did, because Raymond had disobeyed. It was a long, long time before Raymond would go close to a well."

"It must have been the angels watching over him," Rodney spoke up.

"Yes, I'm sure it was," Mother agreed.

"Let's sing the bedtime song," Joanna begged, "the one about angels."

Softly Mother began singing, and the others joined in.

"God is with us, never fear;
Angels are watching o'er me.
His guarding hand is always near,
Angels are watching o'er me.

"As I work and as I play,
Angels are watching o'er me.
They are with me through the day,
Angels are watching o'er me.

"When I lay me down to sleep,
Angels are watching o'er me.
I pray Thee, Lord, my soul to keep;
Angels are watching o'er me.

"All day, all night,
Angels are watching o'er me;"
All day, all night,
Angels are watching o'er me."

"Do you know a story about when God took care of me?" Joanna asked when they had finished singing.

"I know of another time when God watched over some of you children, but let's save that story for tomorrow night," answered Mother, giving her a smile.

Angels Are Watching O'er Me

1, 2–Lily A. Bear
3–Revised, source unknown

Melody source unknown
Four-part music arranged by
Paul M. Landis

1. God is with us, nev - er fear; An - gels are watch-ing o'er me.
2. As I work, and as I play, An - gels are watch-ing o'er me.
3. When I lay me down to sleep, An - gels are watch-ing o'er me.

His guard - ing hand is al - ways near; An-gels are watch-ing o'er me.
They are with me thru the day; An-gels are watch-ing o'er me.
I pray thee, Lord, my soul to keep; An-gels are watch-ing o'er me.

All day, all night, An - gels are watch-ing o'er me.

All day, all night, An - gels are watch-ing o'er me.

29

The Second Day

"Something must have scared your turkeys last night," Tom, one of the boarders remarked the next morning as they were eating breakfast. "I heard an awfully loud commotion in the middle of the night."

"Turkeys!" Raymond exclaimed. "I forgot all about the turkeys this morning." A frown appeared on his forehead. "I don't remember seeing them on their usual perch. I wonder if something happened to them or if they roosted at another place."

"Weren't they on the barn platform?" Mother asked.

"I can't remember seeing them there," Raymond answered thoughtfully. "I'll go see if I can find them after breakfast."

"I'll help you look," Tom offered.

"By the way, I remember hearing a vehicle start up the hill somewhere after the turkeys woke me up," Jack, another boarder, contributed.

After breakfast, Tom, Jack, and Raymond went to look for the missing turkeys. They were not to be found anywhere in the barnyard. "Let's walk up the road to the hill and look around," the men decided.

"Here's a turkey feather." Tom stooped and picked it up as he spoke.

A little farther ahead, more turkey feathers and some blood were strewn over the frost-covered ground.

"Well, I guess we know what happened to the turkeys," Raymond told the men as they turned to walk back. "Thank you for helping me look."

"We didn't mind," Jack answered quickly. "Are you going to try and find out who stole them? Three big turkeys like they were have a lot of good eating on them."

Raymond shook his head. "The Bible

says we should love our enemies and do good to them that hate us, and we are not to return evil for evil," Raymond stated quietly.

The men did not respond, but continued to walk silently down the hill.

"If only Father were here," Raymond thought miserably. "He could explain non-resistance so much better than I." Then, as they neared the bunk house, Raymond said, "Thanks again for helping me look."

"That's all right," Tom answered. Then he turned, and laying his hand on Raymond's shoulder and looking him in the eye, he said, "Always do what you believe; it's the right way." He opened the bunkhouse door and both men disappeared inside.

"Thank You, God, for helping me speak the truth," Raymond breathed as he bounded across the porch and into the house.

"Someone killed our turkeys up on the hill," Raymond informed Mother. "But can you guess what else happened?"

Mother looked questioningly into Raymond's face.

"Jack asked me if we were going to try to find out who did it, and I said, 'No, because the Bible says we should love our enemies and return good for evil' After I told them what the Bible says, neither of them spoke, and I thought I hadn't explained it clearly enough. I was wishing Father were here as he could have told them better. I could hardly believe it when Tom said I should keep on believing like I do, because it's the right way."

"I believe it impressed them more to hear you tell them than if Father would have said it, because you are just a boy. I'm happy, Son, that you were faithful in witnessing to them."

"God helped me, Mother," Raymond stated quietly.

That evening when the dishes were washed and put away, the younger children eagerly gathered around the stove, ready for the promised story. Even Raymond and Martha laid their books aside when Mother began.

"This story took place when we lived on our old farm, beside Swift River. Linda was only three months old, Martha three years, and Raymond five.

"One morning when Father milked the cows he discovered that one cow was missing. All day Father hunted for her, looking among the neighbors' cows and in the woods, but he could find no trace of her. After supper he decided to take the horse and go along the river to see if he could find her there.

"It got later and later; still Father did not come home. I didn't know where he was, and neither could I go and try to find him because I could not leave you children. I prayed, asking God to watch over Father and if it was His will, that he would find the cow, for we were poor, and we needed her.

"You children were all in bed and sleeping, so I went to bed, too, and fell asleep. Sometime later I heard *tap, tap, tap* on the window. Quickly I got out of bed, found it was Father and unfastened the door for him. He asked me to dress and go with him. He harnessed the horse and hitched her to the buggy while I hurriedly got ready. I checked you children to see if you were all right, then went with Father.

"I remember that it was a pitch-black night. Father told me how, when he was walking along the steep river bank, he had heard a noise in the water below. He discovered a beaver's slide, down which the cow had slipped, and since the river was ten feet beneath the steep bank, the cow was unable to climb back up.

"Father had taken the rope off of the horse he was riding and tied the cow's head up out of the water, securing the rope to a tree above. After doing that, he came home and awoke me.

"When we neared the river we unhitched the buggy, took the horse, and walked the rest of the way. I carried a lantern and the block and tackle while Father carried a bale of hay. When we reached the beaver slide, Father secured the block and tackle around a big tree, and using the horse to pull the rope, we were able to get the cow out of the water onto the bottom of the beaver slide.

"The weight of the cow dragged a lot of sand ahead of her, so Father had to go down and dig it away before we could try to pull the cow up the rest of the way.

"Slowly the horse pulled again. The cow was nearly to the top of the slide when one of the ropes broke. How thankful we were that the block and tackle locked so the rest of the ropes held. Father secured her with a chain.

"Since she had been in the water for a long time, the cow was quite chilled. Father and I rubbed her good, covered her with the hay, and left her.

"Over two hours had passed before we got back home. I remember praying often for you little children at home all alone. God answered my prayers, for you were still sleeping peacefully when we arrived home."

"What happened to the poor cow?" Rodney asked when Mother paused.

"Father went back the next morning with feed. He dragged her farther from the bank and rubbed her good again. By that evening the cow was standing up."

"I don't remember hearing that story before," Linda stated. "I would like to go back to that river again sometime."

"We haven't been back to our old farm for a long time," Mother admitted. "It would be nice to go sometime. Now it is bedtime, children, and tomorrow, the Lord willing, Father will be home."

"But I say unto you which hear, Love your enemies, do good to them which hate you" (Luke 6:27).

"See that none render evil for evil unto any man; but ever follow that which is good, both among yourselves, and to all men" (1 Thessalonians 5:15).

30

Third Day

"My, it's cold outside!" Raymond exclaimed when he came in from doing chores the next morning.

"Yes, winter will soon be here to stay," Mother answered. "How thankful we can be that God gave us such a beautiful fall. A few times it turned cold and snowed a little, but it always warmed up again. Now that October is halfway past, we can expect heavy snows any time."

"Should I stay home from school today to stack firewood?" Raymond asked.

Mother looked thoughtfully at Raymond.

"Let me think about it for a little while," she answered. Later, her decision was that Raymond should stay.

"I wish I could stay to help," Linda begged. "Besides, I don't like to go to school—there is no one else in my grade."

"I know, but let's be thankful Anna is in the next grade. You are together at recess and noon, aren't you, Dear?" Mother tried to comfort her.

"I still wish we could go to a Christian school like Uncle Vern's children do," Linda persisted.

"It would be nice, and I hope and pray that someday you children will have that privilege," Mother answered wistfully.

When Linda saw Mother's troubled expression, she wished she had not said anything about staying home from school. "I'll go," she murmured, and hurried to get ready.

As Mother watched the children leave on the bus, her heart yearned for the time when they would have their own church school. But she knew that not everyone in the church felt as she and Father did about it. "Heavenly Father," she silently pleaded, "guide us that we may do Thy will."

"Guess I'll start on the firewood," Raymond said, breaking the silence. "I would like to surprise Father."

"He will appreciate it," Mother smiled.

Off and on during the summer Father and Raymond had sawed firewood, tossing the pieces in a pile beside the sawmill. Raymond took the tractor and wagon to the mill and was soon busy loading wood. *Thud, thud, thud*—the wood hit the wagon as he worked steadily.

"One load ready," he said aloud as he started up the tractor and headed for the house. After that was unloaded, he went back for another load. Long before dinnertime Raymond was hungry and tired, but he was determined to have all the wood at the house before Father came home that night.

Thoughts of Father brought thoughts of the van. Only two more weeks until Raymond would turn fifteen. "I wonder if Father remembers that I'm old enough to get my driver's permit?" he thought as he stopped to rest. How he would enjoy to get behind the steering wheel!

All morning Raymond loaded and

unloaded wood.

"You have gotten quite a bit stacked," Mother praised him when she called him for dinner.

Having a full stomach gave Raymond renewed energy to get back to his job. Slowly the afternoon went by. With deep satisfaction he watched the pile by the sawmill

All morning Raymond loaded and unloaded wood.

dwindle and the woodpile by the house get longer and higher.

"Do you have any more to get?" Martha called to him when she got off the bus. "It looks as if you have really been working today. My, what a big woodpile!"

"There are several more loads," Raymond answered, pleased that she had noticed his hard work. "Do you want to help?"

"I'll help," Martha agreed readily.

"We'll help, too," Linda and Rodney added, "but we need something to eat first. We are hungry."

How much faster the job went with Martha, Linda, and Rodney helping. The last load was stacked before chore time, and when Martha offered to help with the chores, Raymond did not turn down her offer.

It seemed that every muscle ached when Raymond, with the chores finished, walked in for supper. He had not worked so hard since school had started in September.

"This supper surely looks good," Raymond declared, taking his place at the table.

"It smells good, too," Tom added. "By

the looks of the woodpile outside, someone hasn't been lazy today, either."

Raymond smiled at Tom; a happy glow in his heart made Raymond forget his aching muscles. He took a bite of mutton, savoring its goodness. Only Mother knew how to take sheep meat, roast it just right, and then slice it and cover it all with gravy. Even the boarders heartily agreed that the meat and Mother's baking soda biscuits could not be better.

Mother piled a plate with food for Father, then put it in the cook stove warmer so it would be ready when he came home.

"Now what shall we do?" Mother asked the children when the evening's work was completed.

"May we stay up until Father comes?" Rodney asked.

"Unless it gets too late," Mother promised, "but I believe Father will come before too long."

"Why not tell another story?" Joanna suggested eagerly. "I could listen to stories every evening."

"Shall I tell you of a family that had lots of good times together?"

"Yes, do." Joanna climbed up on the rocker arm, waiting for Mother to begin.

"The children in this story had learned it was a lot of fun when everyone helped each other. One day the parents decided they needed another house. It needed to be a warm house so that when winter came they would not be able to feel cold drafts across the floor or icy winds coming through the walls."

"Oh, I know what story you're going to tell," Linda giggled.

"Sh." Mother put her finger to her lips. "The parents decided they could build such a house, for it would take mostly just hard work. But who would be the hard workers? Well, the children decided they would be the hard workers. They carried boards, pounded nails, loaded rocks, shoveled sawdust, and did everything they could to help finish the house."

"Are we the children?" Joanna wanted to know.

"Yes, you are the children," Mother replied, giving her arm a loving pat.

"Tell us more," Joanna begged.

"I don't think I have time," Mother said, her eyes twinkling. "Wouldn't you rather go look out the window and tell me what you see and hear outside?"

Obediently Joanna climbed on a chair and peered out into the darkness. "Oh, Father's here," she squealed. Jumping down, she raced for the door.

"Well, well, did you miss me?" Father teased, giving her a kiss.

"Can we see our van?" Joanna asked breathlessly.

Hurriedly pulling on coats and caps, everyone followed Father outside to the van.

"Just think, it's really our own!" Martha exclaimed as she surveyed the dark blue van.

Raymond climbed into the driver's seat, wondering how it would feel to be able to drive.

"Come inside the van, Mother," Father encouraged. "I want to show you something." Father helped Mother up the big step. He turned on the dome light and the children crowded around to see what Father was going to show.

Father opened a box, revealing something wrapped in newspaper.

"What is it?" Joanna asked, perplexed.

Father unwrapped the newspaper and

took out a package of peas.

"Peas?" Rodney asked.

"Yes. All these boxes contain frozen and canned fruit and vegetables," Father explained.

"For us?" Mother whispered softly in wonderment. "How can we ever thank people?" Tears filled her eyes as she thought of the love their relatives and friends had shown to them.

"God gives us so much," Martha said, speaking the feelings of each one.

"Yes, indeed He does," Father agreed.

While Father ate supper, Raymond and the girls unloaded the boxes of food.

"Did you tell our relatives we had a deepfreeze?" Linda questioned. "Or how did they know?"

"No, but Mother had written to Grandmother that we had gotten one," Father said. "Early this morning before I was ready to leave, Grandmother had gotten up and packed all this frozen food in boxes. It was a surprise to me, too."

"John, just look at all they sent! Peas, corn, beans, even pie cherries." Mother surveyed the packages stacked neatly in the deepfreeze.

"And here are jars of canned pears, peaches, even whole crab apples!" Martha exclaimed. "Umm—I love crab apple fruit."

"It does look nice," Father approved, taking a look. "And when we do our fall butchering the deepfreeze will be almost full."

"It looks beautiful!" Mother declared. "I never expected such a wonderful surprise!" Almost reverently she closed the deepfreeze lid.

"There is a surprise here I never expected to see," Father told them. "The big surprise is in front of the house."

Raymond grinned self-consciously when Father looked at him.

"Thanks so much, Son, for hauling and stacking the firewood. How good it is to be back with my family and to receive such a wonderful welcome."

The happy feeling Raymond had experienced earlier seemed to glow even brighter. "How true it is," he thought contentedly, "that when you help someone else you receive the biggest blessing yourself."

31

Ice Fishing

Raymond slowly walked to the barn in the morning stillness. The only sound he heard was the *crunch, crunch* of his boots against the frost-covered ground. His eyes swept across the landscape. Thick frost covered the ground, trees, fences, and buildings, taking away their drab, pre-winter look.

"How beautiful," Raymond thought as he paused at the barn door. "I'm so glad the weather is finally staying below freezing."

Hurriedly he began the chores, eager to get the work done so Father and he could head for the lake. Ice fishing was always a treat.

Breakfast was finally over, and Raymond slipped into his heavy coat.

"Have a good day, Son," Mother smiled as Raymond opened the door.

Raymond turned and returned Mother's smile. "I hope to. Bye, Mother. Thanks for the good breakfast."

Quickly Raymond shut the door and went to bring the tractor to the house. As he waited for Father, Raymond checked the fishing gear in the wagon. "Hm-m," he murmured to himself, "tubs, net, jigger, axe, rope, weights—I believe we have everything."

"Ready?" Father climbed onto the tractor fender. "We should get started."

The sharp wind slapped against his face and Raymond pulled his collar closer, glad for his warm coat. Over the hum of the tractor motor, Raymond could hear the clatter of the tubs as the wagon bounced over the frozen gravel road. Winding through the forest, the road made its way up one hill, then descended the other side before starting up the next gentle slope.

"Oh, it is good to be out on a morning like this!" Raymond thought as they sped along.

Several miles later Father and Raymond started down the long hill that took them to the shores of Bear Lake. The final curve brought them in view of the smooth, frozen lake stretching from one frost-covered evergreen shore to the next. Raymond slowed down, then eased the tractor onto the lake and drove a short distance before stopping.

"It's good to move around again," Father remarked as he jumped from the tractor, swinging his arms and walking briskly around on the ice. "That wind goes through you. But we'll soon get enough exercise," he decided as he picked up the axe.

A short distance from the wagon he brought his axe down with a swift swing. *Thud! Crack!* The stillness echoed back: *thud, crack!* Again and again Father's axe rang as it chipped away the ice. Finally he broke through to water, and he widened the hole enough to insert the jigger.

Raymond handed the jigger to Father. Father had made their jigger by using a board to which he nailed metal teeth along the upper side and attached a rope to one end.

Father pushed the jigger into the hole, making sure the metal teeth were on top of the water beneath the ice. Holding the rope taut, Father slowly let the jigger float out while jerking the rope with short, sharp jerks, thus making the teeth of the jigger "walk" against the ice.

"Follow the jigger, Son," Father called as he fed out more rope, while constantly keeping the rope taut and continuing the jerking motion.

Raymond walked softly, listening, trying to locate the jigger. Then he dropped on his hands and knees. Yes, he could hear the dull *thud, thud, thud* of the teeth "walking" against the ice. Crawling along, he continued to listen, following the jigger's movements under the ice.

After playing out about one hundred yards of rope, Father called, "Mark the spot now, then come hold this rope."

Raymond laid the axe where he had last heard the jigger and ran to take the rope from Father.

Once again the air rang with sharp hollow cracks as Father chopped the second hole.

"Play out a little more rope now," Father

instructed. Raymond obeyed and soon the jigger floated across the open hole.

"Okay," Father called," you may put the net in."

Slowly Raymond lowered the net while Father steadily pulled the rope through his hole until the net reached him. The net was now in place, and all they had to do was anchor the ends with weights and leave it until late afternoon.

Raymond unhooked the wagon, and then he climbed up beside Father as he drove off the lake and headed through the forest on the logging trail leading to a small sawmill.

"Look!" Father pointed ahead. He slowed the tractor down and stopped. Standing in the middle of the trail was a bull moose, poised as if ready for flight. What a picture! The stately figure was surrounded on either side by frost-shrouded branches. Behind the moose, the narrow trail stretched in a thin line, touching the crystal-clear blue sky. Sensing danger, the moose tossed his mighty antlers and leaped back into the safety of the forest.

That view of one of God's splendid creatures left Raymond awed. "How . . .

how . . . magnificent!" he breathed softly.

"We serve a mighty God." Father spoke quietly as he started the tractor.

The day passed quickly as Father and Raymond tramped the forest, investigating good logging areas. Then it was time to go back and check their net so they could get home before dark.

Once again Father backed the tractor and wagon up to the net. He rechopped the ice holes. Then hooking the rope from the net to the wagon, Father slowly inched the tractor forward.

"My, we're dragging up a lot of water!" Raymond shouted to Father.

Turning to see what Raymond meant, Father took one look at the dark water spreading over the ice. "Hurry, unhook the rope!" he shouted.

Raymond quickly slipped the rope off the wagon hook and Father drove the tractor and wagon to shore. By the time Father stopped the tractor and walked back to the net, the water had disappeared down the hole again."

"What happened? Were we sinking?" Raymond asked in bewilderment.

"Yes, we were," Father replied. "The ice

"My, we're dragging up a lot of water," Raymond
shouted to Father.

won't sink now with just us on it, but the tractor was too heavy. Evidently the ice isn't frozen as solid as I thought, and with the warm sun shining on it this afternoon, it wasn't holding us."

Swiftly Father and Raymond worked, taking the fish out of the net and restringing it. Raymond was anxious to get off the ice. He did not trust it anymore.

At last they were safely on solid ground and traveling homeward. Twilight was gathering when they reached the farm. How inviting the warm, soft glow of the lamplight looked!

After the men recounted the events of the day, Mother spoke softly, "I thought of you today and entrusted you to God. It wasn't that I was uneasy or afraid," Mother explained to the listening children, "but when we pray and ask God for something, we can have rest, knowing that God knows and sees everything."

Father smiled lovingly at Mother. "God does promise that when we ask, we will receive so that our joy may be full."

Later that evening Raymond kept thinking of the conversation at the supper table. "I wonder where Father found that promise in the Bible." He hunted for the verse but could not find it.

"Father?" Raymond ventured hesitantly, for Father was busy studying.

"Yes?" Father looked up questioningly.

"Where does the Bible say, 'Ask, and ye shall receive, that your joy will be full'?"

Father turned in his Bible to John 16 and read verse 24 to Raymond. " 'Hitherto have ye asked nothing in my name. Ask, and ye shall receive, that your joy may be full.' " Father sat quietly for a moment, then asked, "Do you understand what it's saying?"

"Not exactly," Raymond admitted.

"Remember what Mother said at the supper table?" Father paused. "She asked God to keep us and guide us today. She had faith that God would do so, according to His will. So Mother received a blessing or joy, for coming to God in prayer. This joy gave her peace so that she could go about her duties without anxiety, knowing that our heavenly Father is in control of everything. Whatever comes our way, if we seek God and His will, we receive a joy that only God's children can experience."

"I understand now." Raymond smiled his thanks to Father as he stood up and yawned sleepily. In the quietness of his bedroom Raymond thought again about receiving joy. "It is a joy," he breathed gratefully, "to have Christian parents who care."

32

Night Chorus

Mournfully the singers' voices quavered in the distance—rising and falling in volume, then dying away, only to start again in louder chorus.

Bow-wow. Bow-wow. Shep, the faithful sheep dog, barked sharply, letting the distant voices know someone was guarding the sleeping farm.

Linda turned over restlessly in her sleep. Again the eerie notes rose and fell. She snuggled deeper under her blankets, covering her head to shut out the sound, and then she drifted off to sleep again.

Linda awoke again. This time she heard the banging of the stove as Father added more wood.

As Linda lay quietly, wrapped in the warmth of her blankets, she remembered the coyotes she had heard in the night. How she hated coyotes! "If only Father would leave a light lit," she thought. But she did not want to ask as Father would wonder why she wanted a light. She certainly did not want anyone to know that she was afraid of coyotes! "At least they weren't close last night," she comforted herself.

Linda crawled out of bed and stepped onto the icy floor. *Brr*—the house was cold.

"Well, good morning. You're up early!" Father exclaimed in surprise as Linda came and stood close to the stove. He added more wood and adjusted the stove damper.

"I'm cold," Linda shivered, moving closer. Faintly she could hear the crackle of the fire as it started burning. Soon it was blazing merrily, and Linda welcomed the warmth.

"I must begin chores." Father reached for his boots warming by the stove. "Will you call Raymond, please? It's getting daylight."

Linda forgot the coyotes and her fear of them as she sat by the warm fire watching the sky become lighter and lighter, but the next night the chorus came again to pay a visit to the sleeping farm.

Bow-wow. Bow-wow. Shep barked loudly, again awakening Linda. *Bow-wow. Bow-wow.*

Then Linda heard the mournful, eerie notes rising and falling in volume. This time

Linda's skin tingled, and she shivered with fright.

they sounded much closer. Linda's skin tingled, and she shivered in fright when the coyotes howled. Plugging her ears with her fingers she tried to drown out the frightening noise. Only when all was still again did she drift off into a restless sleep.

Once again Linda awoke to hear Father fixing the fire, and she stole out of bed to seek warmth and comfort from the stove.

"Well, good morning, Linda, you're early again." Father looked intently at Linda, perplexed at her early rising.

"Good morning, Father," she murmured as she once more knelt by the stove, listening to the crackling fire. Only when the morning sun spread its light, sending the darkness away, did Linda's fear leave her.

That evening Linda dreaded to go to bed. She tried reading a book, hoping Mother would not notice how late it was becoming.

"Linda, it's past bedtime," Mother reminded her. Reluctantly Linda closed her book and slowly walked to the bedroom.

"I believe something is bothering her," Father remarked to Mother. "The past two mornings, she has gotten up early and has hardly had a word to say."

"I'll talk with her," Mother answered thoughtfully.

That night the moon was bright and round. It bathed the snow-covered farm in a silvery glow. Linda parted the bedroom curtains, taking in the bright moonlight and the peaceful farm yard.

"Why do I always get scared?" Linda asked herself. "But I won't tonight," she resolved with determination, and soon she was fast asleep.

Like the past two nights, the night chorus came again to sing.

Startled, Linda sat up in bed. "Why," her heart pounded wildly, "they are right outside our house!" Quickly covering her head, she plugged her ears and lay shaking with fear as she heard the nerve-wracking wailing.

As all finally became quiet again, she slowly relaxed, but sleep did not come for a long time. When she did fall asleep, Linda dozed restlessly until daybreak; she awoke tense and tired.

"What a way to begin a day," she thought to herself as she wearily climbed out of bed and joined the rest of the family.

Later that Saturday morning, Mother

called to her, "Linda, could you help me tidy up the bedrooms? We will let Martha and Joanna work in the kitchen.

"Dear, what is bothering you?" Mother questioned as she searched Linda's troubled face.

Surprised, Linda glanced at Mother, then burst out, "I can't sleep at night. The coyotes keep me awake, they're so—so scary."

Putting her arm around Linda, Mother asked kindly, "Have you been forgetting to pray?"

"No," Linda shook her head. "Every night I pray when I go to bed; but it doesn't help," she added tearfully. "And every night I tell myself I'm not going to be afraid. But then I am."

"I believe you're afraid because you forget to ask God at the moment you're afraid," Mother spoke tenderly. "When you hear the coyotes, breathe a prayer to God. Then say some memory verses over in your mind, or a song. I'm sure you'll be surprised at how it helps."

"I feel better already," Linda admitted, "just talking with you. I didn't want anyone to know I was afraid," she added sheepishly.

"It never hurts us to admit our weaknesses," Mother went on. "To admit them usually helps us to overcome them. We can't do anything in our own strength but only with God's help. So remember that when you become afraid again; I'm sure He will help you to overcome this fear."

That evening as Linda sat beside their round barrel stove watching the flickering firelight, Father spoke to her. "Do you know the coyotes' habits?"

"No," Linda answered, interested. "Tell me about them."

"As you know, they're night animals, and each pack has its own territory," Father began. "They usually follow game trails, traveling short distances seeking food. That's why we don't always hear them. Sometimes they are here. Sometimes they are there. The last couple of nights they've been pretty close."

"Several days ago they were following a game trail on the other side of the lake, then on Wednesday and Thursday nights they were on this side. Last night they were in the field right behind the barn. And now tonight they'll be past our farm and seem farther away.

"They catch and eat only small animals, like rabbits," Father continued, "and they're very much afraid of humans. Try listening carefully to their mournful howling, and you will learn to love hearing it. The coyote is one of the wild, untamed animals God has created. He has a purpose for them because everything God created, He called good.

"In the light of the full moon at night I have seen coyotes sitting on the hill behind the barn with their faces pointed to the moon, howling mournfully. I love to hear them." Father's eyes twinkled at Linda as he smiled.

Linda returned the smile, knowing she would never be quite as afraid of coyotes again.

33

Vacation Days

"I passed!" Raymond's excited voice betrayed his outward calmness as he showed Mother the treasured driver's permit.

"I'm glad, Son," Mother smiled. Then she thoughtfully continued. "Having your driver's permit will now place a lot of responsibility on you. Whenever you drive you will be responsible for the safety of the vehicle, the safety of those riding with you, and the safety of those you meet on the road." Mother looked up into the eyes of her tall, fast-maturing son. "If you always drive carefully, I'm sure you won't have anything to regret."

"I'll try, Mother," Raymond answered soberly.

Driving seemed to come naturally for Raymond, for he had already spent quite a few years driving tractor. But when the heavy winter snows started, Raymond found that driving the van was quite a bit different than driving the tractor. Often the roads were slippery and snow-covered, or snowdrifts stretching across the road made it hard to tell where the road really was.

"I wish it were spring," Raymond thought impatiently as he slowly drove out of the church yard onto the snowy roads one Sunday. "Then I wouldn't have to worry about landing in the ditch, but at least Father lets me drive even if I do have to go slowly," he consoled himself.

"Only one more week till Christmas vacation!" Linda exclaimed joyously from the back seat. "It is going to be wonderful to have two whole weeks of vacation. Father, could we go sleigh riding sometime while we are home? I miss using our covered sleigh," she added wistfully.

"So do I," Rodney agreed with her. "But

I like our van, too."

"I would much rather ride in the van," Martha stated.

"Me, too," Joanna agreed with Big Sister.

"Oh, no. Last winter was much more fun when we went to church with our horses," Linda insisted.

"Do you think we could have a sleigh ride?" Rodney asked again.

"I believe we might be able to," Father smiled. "But I'm afraid our days of using the covered sleigh are over. It would need quite a bit of fixing to be usable. You may have to settle for a ride on the logging sleigh."

"That's okay," Rodney answered agreeably. "Just so we have a sleigh ride again."

The first day of vacation dawned, but all was darkness, for once again the longest night was upon them. Even though darkness covered the farm, all was bright and cheery inside the house. Mother was cooking dinner, and by late morning the smell of chicken and dressing seeped through the oven door to mingle with the delicious odors of the fresh pumpkin pies cooling on top of the stove warmer.

"We are thankful for the opportunity to keep the lodgers, but it is nice that they are gone for a week and our family is alone," Father observed.

Mother finished mixing the biscuit dough, then handed the bowl to Martha so she could roll out the biscuits. "Let's see," she said, thinking aloud, "chicken and dressing, gravy, biscuits, red beet pickles, and pie. I believe dinner will be ready as soon as the biscuits are baked."

"I'm so hungry!" Rodney complained. "The whole house smells good enough to eat."

"It won't be long until we can eat," Mother consoled him.

"Your delicious dinner tasted even better than it smelled," Father complimented Mother as he pushed back his plate. "Now I think this first day of vacation calls for something special—like a sleigh ride."

"A sleigh ride! Yes!" the children chorused eagerly.

When the early afternoon sun shone bright and clear, the family bundled up for their sleigh ride in the frosty, sparkling outdoors.

"What fun," Linda sighed as the sleigh sped along spraying fine white snow from the runners.

Father had harnessed up faithful Betsy, and even she seemed to be enjoying herself. Every now and then she would snort and toss her head as if to say, "This is fun! I could pull you a long way!"

When Betsy slowed down to a gentle trot, Martha tried to reach the low, snow-covered branches hanging out over the trail. Birds chirped noisily and flew to higher branches as the sleigh riders drew near, scolding at them for intruding on their territory. A snowshoe rabbit scurried into the thick underbrush.

"There is Raymond's shack," Rodney called. They could see the broken wall and roof with the snow-ladened tree top still lying across the top.

All too soon twilight began to gather and it was time to head for home. Passing the silent, snowy sawmill, Father remarked, "I remember this same horse and sleigh taking Raymond and me over this trail almost a year ago. Then we were entirely in God's hands, for the quick snowstorm had blotted out everything, and we were traveling in a world of swirling darkness."

"I'm so glad it was beautiful today," Martha commented. She, too, remembered the time Father and Raymond had been lost and the fear for them that she had had.

"Doesn't that look like David's father's truck?" Rodney asked when they arrived home again.

"I believe it is," Father replied.

"Looks like your family is having a nice time," David's father called to them when they stopped.

"Yes, we are," Father called back cheerily.

Mother and the girls went into the house while David and Raymond unhitched Betsy and took her into the barn.

"Father came to see if it would suit your parents for me to stay with you for two days," David informed Raymond. "Grandmother is in the hospital, and Father and Mother want to go and see her."

"Good," Raymond told his friend enthusiastically. "I know it will be all right with Father. It will be a lot of fun to have you here for a couple of days."

Before the family had finished eating supper, David's father brought him over to stay. That evening as Father sat by the stove carving a new gun stock, he said, "How would you boys like to do a little wood carving? I'll show you something simple."

Selecting a piece of soft pine from his wood scraps, Father drew the outlines for two pliers on it. Then he cut the wood in two pieces and handed David and Raymond each a piece.

"Whittle out the wood around the outline, and the plier's center hole," he instructed.

The boys opened their jack knives and set to work, carving carefully until they were finished.

"Now I will show you how to cut away the wood so that the pliers will open and close," Father told them.

The boys watched, puzzled. How could the pliers be moveable when they were one solid piece of wood?

Father notched out two depressions on both sides of the pliers. Turning the pliers on its side, he cut a *V*-shaped notch beside each depression. Very carefully he slipped the tip of his knife from depression to depression, working it just under the surface of the wood to make an opening. Turning the pliers over, he did the same thing on the other side. Last, Father cut open the top of the pliers, then opened and closed the pliers handles.*

"Oh-h-h!" David exclaimed. "A wooden pliers that really works!"

"Can you boys each make another one?" Father asked.

"Sure," they responded, eager to try.

Carefully David and Raymond worked, and before long they each had the second pliers opening and closing.

"We will have to sand them smooth," Raymond remarked, "then they will look really nice."

"Better leave that for tomorrow," Father told them. "It's bedtime now."

The next day passed quickly as the boys helped in the barn and shop. They even found

---

*Detailed instructions for making this small, interesting pliers that really works (along with measurements and drawings), can be found at the back of this book.

time to snowshoe down to the bottomless lake in the daylight hours.

Mother prepared an early supper as they were planning to go and sing for several shut-in neighbors that evening.

"Let's stop first and visit Freddie Rains' mother," Father suggested when they were ready to leave. "We haven't seen her for quite a while."

Knock, knock. Father knocked at the door of the red, paint-splashed log house while the family waited in the van.

Bow-wow-wow. Two big dogs barked viciously at Father's heels.

Slowly the house door swung open, revealing the tall, husky figure of Freddie Rains. After an exchange of friendly greetings, Father motioned for the family to come. Cautiously they walked toward the small cabin, keeping their eyes on the big, snarling dogs.

"Get back!" Freddie yelled, swinging his fist at one of the dogs. "Get back!" The two dogs slunk away into the shadows.

"Come in, come in," Freddie's mother called from her bed in the kitchen. "I'm so glad you came," she said, her eyes lighting up.

Shyly the children shook hands with the invalid, then quietly waited while their parents visited. "Would you like us to sing for you?" Father asked after a while.

"Yes, yes," Freddie's mother nodded.

Raymond passed out the song books they had brought along and soon the sweet music of God's love filled the dreary home, bringing hope and cheer.

"Do come again," Mrs. Rains urged. "You are welcome any time."

"We have time for one more stop," Father remarked when everyone was in the van again. "Where will it be?"

"I would like to see the two Myers sisters," Mother proposed in kindly tones. "We haven't been there for quite some time."

"A good suggestion," Father agreed.

The van's headlights pierced the darkness as they passed Bear Lake, giving them a brief glimpse of the trees bordering the lake's edge. Ahead wound the white snowy road twisting through the forest, climbing one small hill, then disappearing around a curve.

"I see the Myer's house," Rodney called

when he spotted two big wagon wheels marking the driveway.

Father turned into the driveway and stopped beside a tiny, trim cottage. The shoveled walk led them to the door which opened before Father even had time to knock.

"Do come in," one of the white-haired sisters welcomed them warmly.

Inside, the cottage was even more picturesque than outside. Quaint furniture adorned the rooms; everywhere were home-made doilies, afghans, pictures, and interesting knick-knacks, while beautiful green plants filled the windows. The two sisters, whose eyes twinkled in delight at having visitors, seemed to bubble with happiness.

Swiftly the time passed as they visited and sang for the two widowed sisters.

"Take these goodies for the children," their hostesses said, thrusting a bag of chocolate candies into Mother's hand when at last the family rose to go. "And come back again; come back again. We enjoyed the singing so much."

"I love to go there," Martha sighed contentedly. "Those two old ladies are as dear and interesting as their little house."

"Their house is surely different than Rains'," Rodney added. "Rains' is so dark and gloomy inside. I'd rather sing for the Myers."

"But Mrs. Rains enjoyed our visiting and singing, too," Father responded. "Remember how she thanked us and urged us to come again? We don't want to be partial and only visit those who have nicer things. Christ was especially kind and compassionate to the less fortunate."

"I feel sorry for Mrs. Rains having to lie in bed so much," Linda remarked warmly.

"Yes," Mother agreed. "She maybe needs even more sunshine brought into her life than the Myers sisters do."

"Well—I enjoyed this evening," David spoke up from the back seat. "It is the first time I've ever done something like this and . . . and it has done me good."

Letters

Mother's hands shook as she read the short letter from Uncle Verns. Slowly she read it over again to make sure she was reading it right.

Dear Johns,

Greetings of love in our Savior's Name.

We want to write and tell you about a job opening with the District Crop Irrigation System. Mr. Ruth, the head man, talked with Vern yesterday and wondered if he knew of an experienced man. Right away Vern thought of John since he did that type of work for several years before you moved north; and we also knew of your desire to send your children to a Christian school.

A small rent-free, twenty-acre farm with house, garage, and barn go with the job. The farm is two miles from our place on the opposite side of our road.

Vern told Mr. Ruth he would let you know right away, and Mr. Ruth said he was willing to wait two weeks for an answer before trying to find someone else.

We will be praying for you as you seek God's will in this matter.

Verns

Numbly, Mother sat down, trying to comprehend everything in the letter. Leave their northern home? Move back to her girlhood community? And a Christian school only several miles from Verns?

Mother thought of the struggles to feed and clothe the family when the crops were completely destroyed by hail. Different years they had worked hard only to see the grain flattened.

She thought of the hard, back-breaking work they had done to build the warm house they were now living in. She remembered, too, the joys of working together, of God's wonderful answers to prayer, and of His protection in this rugged land they had called home for the past fourteen years.

She thought of the dear friends they would leave behind if they would move. She thought also of her husband's love for this wild, untamed country and of his hard labor to clear land for farming.

Mother rose from her chair, went into the bedroom, and shut the door. There on her knees she pleaded with God to show them plainly His will.

"Two weeks," she whispered to herself. "Two weeks isn't a very long time."

Together Father and Mother sought God's will, and before the two weeks were up they both felt that God was leading them to sell their farm and take the job at Banks.

Ten days after sending their reply to Mr. Ruth, Father received a letter stating that he was accepted for the job. He was to begin work the first of May.

"Listen to this," Father said as he read to Mother Mr. Ruth's closing statement: " 'Although I haven't interviewed you personally, your references are excellent. So I am hiring you on faith.' "

"That goes to show that now, as always, God is in control," Mother stated softly.

"We have only two months until May," Father said, looking at the calender. "A lot will need to be done in that time."

Excitement filled the house when the children found out they were moving close to Uncle Verns, and yet in quiet moments, the older ones had misgivings about leaving all that was familiar.

"O Martha," Dorothy wailed when she found that her friend was leaving, "what will I do without you?"

"I'll miss you, Raymond," David spoke awkwardly. "You are the only person I have to chum with."

March flew by as Father and Mother sorted through their belongings, getting ready for the farm sale. When April arrived, the warm spring winds blew, melting the snow and driving away the sharp cold. With the sale day nearly upon them, the family worked early and late getting machinery, tools, logs, fence posts, and animals ready to sell. Gratefully, they relaxed the evening before the sale, thankful that everything was in readiness.

But God had other plans, for all night long, big snowflakes silently drifted down, blanketing the farm in four inches of wet, heavy whiteness.

"I can hardly believe this!" Father stood by a window and shook his head in wonder at the white, snow-covered farm that greeted his eyes. "Mother, come and see something beautiful," he called.

"What?" Mother exclaimed in amazement when she saw the snow-laden outdoors. "It is beautiful, but the sale—"

" 'For as the heavens are higher than the earth, so are my ways higher than your ways, and my thoughts than your thoughts,' " Father quoted. "Although we don't understand, God has a purpose in canceling our sale today."

The sale was planned for the following Wednesday, and all day the sun shone brightly. By evening everything was sold except one milk cow they wanted to keep until they moved.

How different it was to go to the empty barn and milk one cow. No horses whinnied their welcome when the barn doors squeaked open. All was silent in the sheep barn, too. Even the lodgers had taken their bunkhouse and left to work at some other place.

Father and Raymond cleaned the barns so all would be ready for the new owners. Then Father received another letter from Mr. Ruth. Could he come two weeks earlier? They needed him due to unexpected complications that had developed along the water canals. In one week Father would need to leave. He would return in a few weeks for the family, who would, in the meantime, be packing the household things.

"Everything has happened so quickly," Mother told Father the evening before he left for Banks. "But it is comforting to know God has planned every detail. Even our farm sold before we advertized it."

"Yes," Father answered sincerely. "God's ways are marvelous—'past finding out'."

We left our home so dear to all
In answer to God's call.
He called us to another land;
We were beneath His caring hand.

How sweet the promise we had claimed,
That God would be the same.
It makes no diff'rence where we'll live:
The same great love, our God will give.

So serve Him faithfully each day,
And live the Bible way.
Then you'll have peace, and want to share
That you are daily in God's care.

Moving

"Father's coming! Father's coming!" Joanna sang in excitement. She skipped from room to room, weaving among the boxes scattered everywhere for last-minute packing.

How they had all missed Father these past two weeks. Things did not seem right when he was not at home—but tonight he would arrive home in time for supper, the Lord willing.

Joanna could hardly wait to see him, and the more she thought about it, the more she wondered whether she would remember him.

"Raymond," she burst out unexpectedly.

Raymond jumped. He had been checking through his boxes, unaware that Joanna was standing beside him.

"I can hardly remember Father. Will he remember me?" Her anxious face peered up at him.

"Of course, Father will know you," Raymond laughingly assured her. "Now run along so I can finish here since Father should be home in less than half an hour."

"Goody, goody," Joanna squealed. "He's been gone so long."

"Yes, he has," Raymond soberly agreed. "And we've all missed him. Now be a good girl and run outside and take one last swing ride."

After Joanna left, Raymond thought about the good friend he would leave behind. He thought about the hills, the trees, and logging with Father. There would be no hills, no acres and acres of towering pine trees— just flat, wide-open spaces.

Yet Raymond was anxious to go, to make new friends, to explore a new country. "Really," he thought, "I'm probably as excited as Joanna, only I don't jump around about it."

Raymond closed the last box, then sat wondering if there was anything else he ought to do. He realized suddenly how tired he was. The past two weeks had been busy ones.

Then he heard Joanna outside calling excitedly, "Father's here, Father's here! He's coming up the lane. Oh, I see him, I see him!"

Raymond joined the others outside as they waited for Father to stop. After happy greetings, everyone sat down to the waiting supper. Father wanted to load the trailer before dark and begin the journey to Banks as soon as it was loaded, so there was little time for talking.

After the meal, while Martha and Linda washed, dried, and packed the dishes, Father, Raymond, and Mother loaded the small two-wheeled trailer. Into it went their clothing, bedding, beds, chairs, and other small household items. This was all they were taking with them. Everything else had been sold or given away.

Dusk was beginning to gather and the trailer was almost loaded when a car slowed and turned into the lane. It was followed by others, and Raymond could see several more sets of lights coming down the hill. What could it mean?

The first car stopped and Raymond recognized the minister and his family. Then he saw the Martin car, and the Wilfords, and other of their neighbors.

"They've all come to say good-by," Raymond thought, surprised. "There's David!" Raymond sprang down from the trailer and hurried to David's side.

Everyone crowded into the empty house and the women were soon busy passing around cookies and a cold drink.

Then someone started singing, "Where He may lead me I will go, / For I have learned to trust Him so." Raymond felt a lump in his throat, and he could hardly sing. Several more hymns were sung and when "God be with You till we meet again," was begun, he had to blink back the tears.

Martha glanced at Dorothy and both girls choked up with tears and could not sing.

Then Brother Wayne spoke. "It is comforting to know that whether we live here or elsewhere, we can still serve the same God, and God's children are all brothers and sisters in Christ. Now before we part, let us pray together for Brother John and his family, that God would give them safety as they travel to their new home. Let us continue to pray for one another that we each would live faithfully for God, wherever we are."

As heads were bowed in prayer, Brother Wayne asked God's protection for the traveling family. He prayed that they would be a blessing in their new community. Raymond silently prayed that the unsaved neighbors who were there among them, would learn to love God, too.

Good-bys were said. Willing hands loaded the deepfreeze into the back of the van and placed all the frozen food inside. Then everyone was gone.

While Father made a last thorough check to see that everything was in readiness to leave, the weary, excited children crowded into the van and found places to settle down and sleep. Mother and Raymond waited for Father on the front seat. Finally, Father took the driver's seat, and they were on their way.

"Do you think you can drive for awhile, Raymond?" Father requested, after driving for several hours. He had already driven many hours that day, and weariness was overtaking him.

"Sure; I'll be careful," Raymond quickly responded.

"Drive carefully, Son, and go slowly—not over thirty-five miles an hour. Remember, we're pulling a heavy load," he advised.

To Raymond it seemed they were just creeping along, yet he was glad Father trusted him. Silently they drove on and on. The night seemed endless.

An hour had passed when Raymond saw a road construction sign. "Oh, no," he groaned, slowing down even more. "I hope this doesn't last long." Then the black top road ended and they were on a gravel road.

The change woke Father up. "Is something wrong?" he asked sleepily.

"No. It's just road construction, so I slowed down," Raymond answered.

"Guess I forgot about this stretch," Father replied. "But I don't believe it lasts very long."

Soon they were back on the pavement again, and Raymond increased his speed. Then, noticing a road flare, he slowed down again.

"I wonder what that flare was for," he said aloud, when the road continued on smoothly. Seeing nothing, he increased his speed.

All of a sudden right in front of him, Raymond saw a ridge of gravel. Slamming on the brakes, he swerved to avoid hitting it.

"Hang on to the steering wheel, Son. Don't step on the brakes. Let the van slow itself," Father tensely gave instructions.

The van started swaying. It was tipping.

The van started swaying. It was tipping. It was going to turn over!

It was going to turn over! Then, with a sharp jolt, it landed back on all four wheels. At the same time they heard a sickening *crunch, bang;* abruptly, still rocking back and forth, the van stopped.

Raymond was shaking so badly he could hardly shut the ignition off.

"Thank God we had the loaded deep-freeze inside the van. It kept it from rolling over," Father quietly told the silent family. "I'm going to see how much damage is done."

When Father returned, he reported, "The trailer broke loose from the van and rolled over. Leave the turn signals on. I'm going to walk ahead to find a farm house."

"Why did this have to happen?" Raymond questioned Mother as he hid his face in his arms on the steering wheel. "If only I hadn't been driving."

"Don't blame yourself, Son," Mother answered kindly. "God has a purpose for everything that He allows. We don't need to understand, but only to accept such things while still praising our heavenly Father.

"We have a lot to be thankful for. No one was hurt, and the van was not wrecked. When the van tipped, if it would have tipped in the opposite direction, the deepfreeze would have slid on the children who were sleeping beside it. Yes, Raymond, we have much to be thankful for."

Time passed slowly while they waited for Father. When Father returned, he was with a wrecker.

"You are going to need new parts," the mechanic told Father after he had inspected the situation. "Why doesn't your family come along back to my garage where it will be more warm and comfortable. It may take a while to fix the trailer hitch."

Again time passed slowly as Mother and the children waited in the strange garage while Father and the mechanic went to make the repairs. An hour later, they were relieved to hear the sound of the wrecker and see the van's lights following with the fixed trailer.

"Well, everything is ready to go again," Father announced.

Once more they started traveling through the darkness. How the hours dragged by through the rest of the night and during the next day. Late in the afternoon Father announced, "Watch carefully now, for as soon as we turn the corner up ahead, you'll be able to see our place.

Linda, Rodney, and Joanna pressed their faces against the window, eagerly watching for the first glimpse.

"Do you see the yellow house and barn?" he asked. "That is our place."

Father turned in the lane and stopped. The children scrambled out. With wide eyes they tried to take in the strange appearance of this new country. A short distance from the house was a garage and small barn. And beyond them, and in every direction, they could see for miles and miles. The neighbors' houses seemed so close, and the clumps of trees dotting the landscape marked many other farms.

As Father unlocked the door to their new home, Raymond realized that a door was also being unlocked for all of them to a new life. A new home, a new country, a new church, a new school, and new friends.

They were in the house only a few minutes when Father called everyone together. "Children," he spoke earnestly, "we all remember how God so wonderfully cared for us in our old home. And again while we traveled here, He spared us from harm. As we live in our new home, let us never forget that God will care for us here, too, as we serve Him faithfully.''

With grateful hearts the family knelt in the bare, unfurnished living room to offer praise to their heavenly Father for His never-ending care.

Directions for Making Wooden Pliers

1. Use a piece of pine (or other soft wood)
   6″ × 1/2″ × 1 1/2″.
2. Trace pliers pattern; use jackknife, sabre, or coping saw for cutting.
3. Round edges of handles with jackknife.
4. Sand pliers smooth.
5. Cut out 1/8″ deep depressions A and B, on both front and back of pliers (Patterns I and II).
6. Turn pliers on side. Cut out a *V*-shaped notch in the center of each side (Patterns I and III). The notch must go through to the opening on notch C, and through to handle on notch D.
7. Use tip of knife blade to carefully cut from bottom of depression A to bottom of depression B, shaving away just enough wood so pliers can be opened.
8. Slit open the top.

Pattern I

(front view)

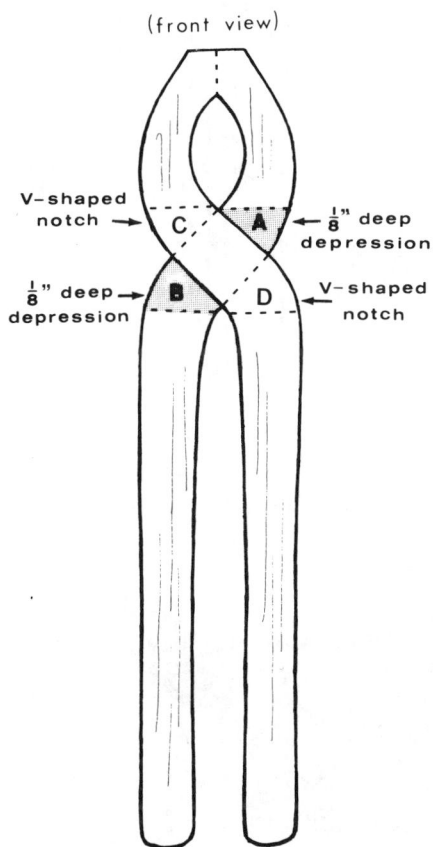

V-shaped notch → C A ← $\frac{1}{8}$" deep depression

$\frac{1}{8}$" deep depression → B D V-shaped notch

Pattern II

(back view)

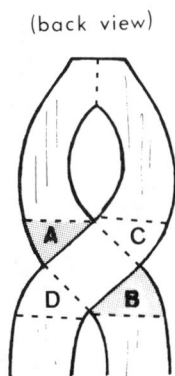

A C

D B

Pattern III

(side views)

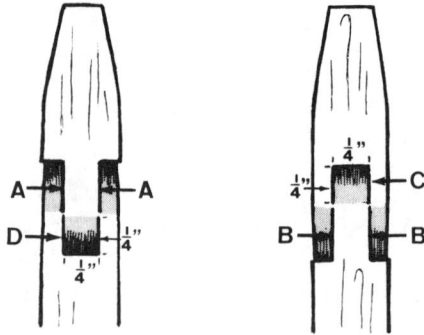

Pattern IV

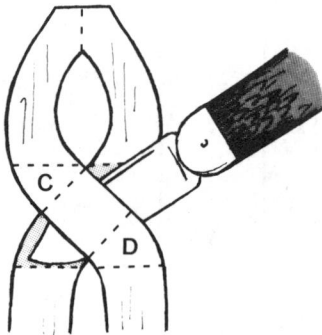

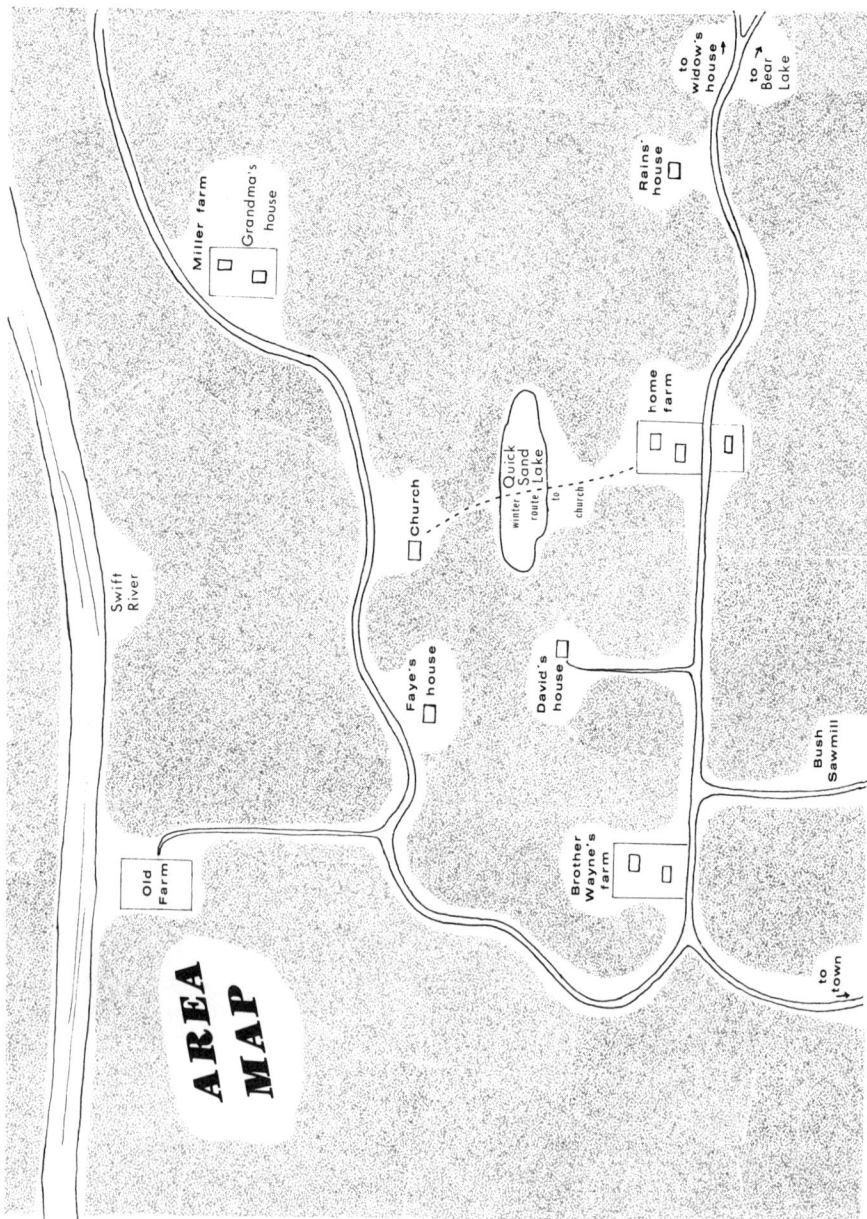

AREA MAP

Old Farm

Swift River

Miller farm

Grandma's house

Rains house

to widow's house

to Bear Lake

church

Quick Sand Lake

winter route to church

home farm

Faye's house

David's house

Brother Wayne's farm

Bush Sawmill

to town

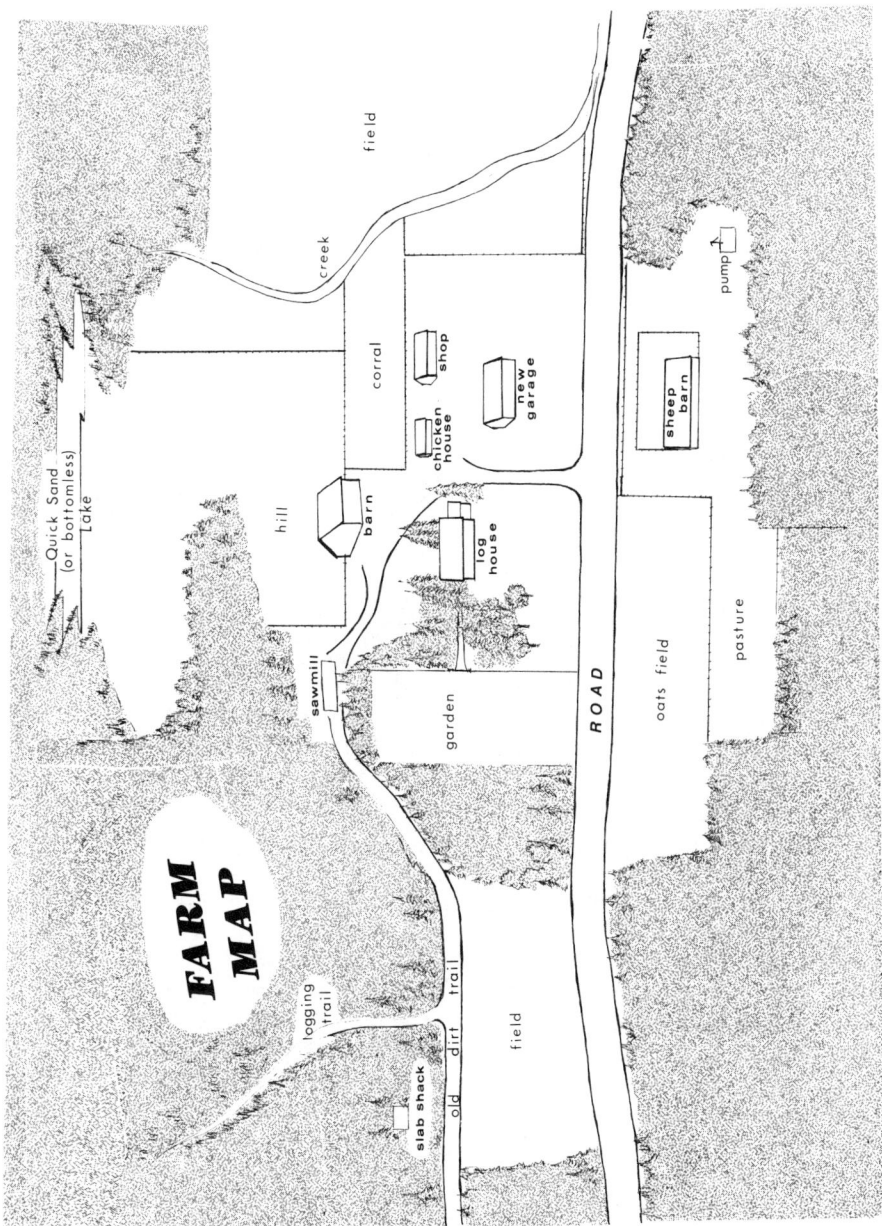

FARM MAP

Quick Sand
(or bottomless)
Lake

field

creek

hill

corral

shop

chicken
house

new
garage

barn

log
house

sawmill

garden

pump

sheep
barn

ROAD

oats field

pasture

logging
trail

old dirt trail

slab shack

field